PRAISE FOR
THE INNOVATOR'S MINDSET

"An inspiring book with a compelling message: why innovation is necessary and possible in education. Educator George Couros illustrates how to unleash talents in a culture of creativity through innovation."

—**YONG ZHAO**, Professor, University of Oregon and author of World Class Learners: Educating Creative and Entrepreneurial Students

"Every educator needs an innovation mindset in today's world. *The Innovator's Mindset* is the 'how to' guide on moving from an industrial to an innovative model of schooling. It is the combination of George's passion for learning and his practical advice for teachers. I always have something to learn from George Couros."

—**GREG WHITBY**, Executive Director of Schools, Catholic Education, Diocese of Parramatta

"George is a wonderful example of not only a networked leader, but a very accessible one as well. The ideas expressed here are ones he lives and derives from listening to others. What George does so well is connect these ideas and bring them to the essentials of teaching and learning. Whether you're a classroom teacher, superintendent, or parent, you'll find something in here that will help you rethink and refocus your efforts. As an added bonus, because of George's willingness to connect, the book is not an end but a beginning of conversations you can have with George and many of the great educators mentioned in this book."

—**DEAN SHARESKI**, Community Manager, Discovery Education

"In this book, George Couros draws an uncanny parallel to the traits that enabled his father to succeed as a post-war immigrant to Canada and the traits that we as educators must adopt in 2015. His father had to be nimble and agile and always eager to learn. Similarly, we need to adopt the "innovator's mindset" that will be so essential to our students becoming effective citizens in the rapidly changing world in which they live. This book is an excellent read for educators who are eager to walk alongside students as they develop this mindset."

—**ANGELA MAIERS**, Educator, Author, Speaker, and Founder of Choose2Matter

"*The Innovator's Mindset* is a must-read for anyone interested in changing the way we approach learning in our schools. With numerous examples of practical strategies that school leaders can implement tomorrow, George has created a guide to help infuse innovative practices in schools and classrooms. The questions for the reflection at the end of each chapter are perfect entry points into school-wide or community-wide conversations about the types of learning environments that our students need. If you are an educator concerned with ensuring compliance, then step away from this book. However, if you are an educator interested in how school leaders can build relationships within their school or district that will lead to higher-level pursuits for all learners, this book will become a critical piece of your learning library. As George states, 'Relationships are the most important element of schools.' If you concur, grab this book for yourself and others in your school community and start reading now."

—**PATRICK LARKIN**, Assistant Superintendent for Learning, Burlington Public Schools

"George Couros has the ability to challenge what you didn't even realize needed to be challenged. He does it deliberately, thoughtfully, and instinctively. These challenges result in a perceptive and practical book--one that will change how you "do" education. More importantly, he inspires you to WANT to be better than you are. If you've seen George present, then you know there is no better story teller than he, and this book is no different. He can make you cry in one sentence, and laugh out loud in the next. From that emotion comes the impetus for change—real change, that will impact educators and students around the globe. If you are looking for a book to help initiate conversations on innovation and challenge the status quo and are unsure where to turn, *The Innovator's Mindset* is the answer. From the "why" to the more applicable "what," he talks you through, step by step, a way to make change happen. I, for one, am a better leader for it. You can't help but be motivated by the simple truths and examples shared. These are real examples from teachers and leaders in classrooms today who are accomplishing the basics and so much more. In a system that measures through standardized lines, these suggestions will take you far beyond what you think you could accomplish and, more importantly, show how to take your students with you."

—**AMBER TEAMANN**, Principal, Wylie ISD

The INNOVATOR'S Mindset

Empower Learning, Unleash Talent, and Lead a Culture of Creativity

George Couros

THE INNOVATOR'S MINDSET
© 2015 by George Couros

This book is available at special discounts when purchased in quantity for use as premiums, promotions, fundraising, and educational use. For inquiries and details, contact us: shelley@daveburgessconsulting.com.

Published by Dave Burgess Consulting, Inc.
San Diego, CA
http://daveburgessconsulting.com

Cover Design by Genesis Kohler
Editing and Interior Design by My Writers' Connection

Library of Congress Control Number: 2015953036
Paperback ISBN: 978-0-9861554-9-9
Ebook ISBN: 978-0-9861554-8-2

First Printing: October 2015

CONTENTS

PUBLISHER'S FOREWORD

Buzzwords crowd the educational reform movement like buzzards circling a decaying carcass. Many have become enamored with—and lost to—a culture of clichés and a penchant for platitudes. Perhaps no word is a better example of this than *innovation*. Its frequent use and misuse has led to the loss of much of its power. However, a true spirit of innovation is exactly what our educational system needs to crush complacency, stomp the status quo, and forge a path into a future that is perpetually in flux.

The Innovator's Mindset: Empower Learning, Unleash Talent, and Lead a Culture of Creativity by George Couros is the manifesto we have been waiting for to lead us out of this jungle of jargon and into the rarefied air of real change. Don't be disappointed that there is no map, no step by step plan to take you to the educational Promised Land. Change isn't something that comes with a checklist. We live in a world where the winds and the sea are constantly shifting and the treasure is never hidden in the same location twice.

Instead, what you hold is a compass. This book is about creating the mindset, the culture, and the relationships to empower the people in your system to be willing and able to trim the sails and set a new course in any kind of weather and in any kind of conditions.

This book is a starting point, the opening of a discussion, an embracing of the idea that we are all learners walking this path together, each of us with our own stories and unique challenges. George seamlessly weaves personal anecdotes, real-world examples from powerful practitioners, and thought-provoking questions designed to push educators to question conventional wisdom into a *tour de force* that is, quite simply, a game changer.

If reading this book makes you uncomfortable, *fantastic*!

If reading it forces you to question long-held and dear beliefs, *wonderful*!

But, if you read this book and it does nothing to change your practice, we failed. Inspiration without implementation is a waste. The inevitability of change is not to be feared but embraced. As George so eloquently says, "Change is an opportunity to do something amazing."

This is your opportunity to make innovation "go viral" system-wide. This is your opportunity to design schools that value creation over compliance and making over memorizing. This is your opportunity to connect with a community of colleagues who are committed to sharing their trials and triumphs, their problems and progress in the knowledge that we are all on the same team to help students win in the game of life.

I have heard George speak. I've seen how well his message resonates and the effect it has on his audience. My great hope for this book was that it approximates the impact of hearing him live and, in my opinion, mission accomplished. There is an authenticity to his message that is powerfully persuasive. Perhaps his greatest gift is how he can simultaneously prod you and pull you, forcing you out of your comfort zone while making you feel as if he is holding your hand and walking with you the whole way.

The journey starts here. And yes, school can be amazing.

DAVE BURGESS
President, Dave Burgess Consulting, Inc.
Author of the *New York Times* bestseller *Teach Like a Pirate* and
co-author of *P is for Pirate*

INTRODUCTION

Once you stop learning,
you start dying.

-Albert Einstein

When I was about six years old, my dad brought home this crazy new device called a "VCR." It had two different components: one for playing a tape (luckily, he bought VHS and not Beta) and the other for setting the timer to record TV shows. He later added a camera. With this "mobile technology" that allowed him to move as far as the extension cord would reach, he took videos of my three siblings and me. Starring in home movies was fun back then, and we now cherish the memories my dad preserved. If he wasn't willing to buy and learn that new technology, I wonder what we would have missed out on. How much of our childhood would we have forgotten?

My dad passed away in March 2013. Until the day he died, he continually tried and learned new things. Whether it was signing up for email, even though he could barely read, or connecting with his kids and grandkids through Facebook, because that is where he knew he would find us, my dad embodied Einstein's maxim: "Once you stop learning, you start dying."

Looking back, it's remarkable to see how much he accomplished after starting life with so little. Growing up during a civil war in Greece, he left school after second grade and later fought in the war. In his twenties, he left Greece to seek new opportunities in Canada. With less than twenty dollars in his pocket, he took a boat across the Atlantic to a country with a radically different climate from that of his home country. He couldn't read or write Greek or English, nor was he able to speak French or English (the two official languages of Canada). Despite a lack of formal education, language barriers, and the countless obstacles he faced as an immigrant, my dad worked his way up from being a dishwasher, to salad chef, to chef, and, eventually, to owning a restaurant for almost thirty years with my mom. He went through all those dramatic changes to create opportunities for his family and himself.

My parents' story is not unique. We often forget the changes our families went through to give us the opportunities we have today—to leave the world a better place. In the same way, our job as educators is to provide new and better opportunities for our students.

Change is an opportunity to do something amazing. My dad understood that. Yet, within the institution of education, there is often a reluctance to embrace the new opportunities. We complain about switching from Microsoft Word to Google Docs, not because it would be worse, but because it is change. And even in schools that have the latest technology, teachers and administrators use that advanced equipment to do the same things they did before. A tool that could change education for the better—a laptop, tablet, or interactive white board—too often ends up becoming the equivalent of a thousand-dollar pencil.

Superintendent John Carver once told me he believes the world is at a "printing press" time in history. Technology affords us opportunities we did not have before. John also commented that we need to rethink the role of schools in education as well as how they operate. He's right. If we don't really think about the way we teach, and, more importantly, how both educators and students learn, we will *all* miss out on the opportunities that lie in front of us. School will continue to look the same as it did when we attended, only in a digital format.

Right now we have many twenty-first-century schools with twentieth-century learning. From an outsider's perspective, they look great.

 CHANGE IS AN OPPORTUNITY TO DO SOMETHING AMAZING. #InnovatorsMindset

One-to-one technology ratios woo students and impress the administration and teachers at neighboring schools. Inside too many of these tech-equipped schools are many uninspired students who believe traditional education is irrelevant. Consider this: students have access to better resources online than what teachers could possibly offer. If schools are only about content and information, that reality poses a threat to educational facilities. If, for example, a student wants to learn about space, she doesn't ask her teacher what space is like. She visits NASA.gov to read blogs by astronauts and scientists. She may even connect with astronauts, such as Commander Hadfield, directly through Twitter. In a powerful video titled "An Open Letter to Educators," university dropout Dan Brown shares some poignant thoughts about why we, as educators, must change not only our tools but also our approach to teaching :

> It is clear to the world that something just isn't working with institutional education, and most people...say, "We need to change institutional education!" But to the educators of the world, I am here today to say that I disagree. You don't need

to change anything. You simply need to understand that the
world is changing, and, if you don't change with it, the world
will decide that it doesn't need you anymore.[1]

You may not agree with everything Dan says in his video, and that's okay. What I hope you will agree with is that there is a clear need for innovation in education. Without innovation, organizations—including educational facilities—cease to exist. If education's leaders refuse to evaluate and stay in touch with students' needs, our institutions will fail, just like businesses that don't keep up with changing customers' needs.

Inspiration is one of the chief needs of today's students. Kids walk into schools full of wonder and questions, yet we often ask them to hold their questions for later, so we can "get through" the curriculum. We forget that our responsibility isn't solely to teach memorization or the mechanics of a task but to spark a curiosity that empowers students to learn on their own.

To wonder.

To explore.

To become leaders.

We forget that if students leave school less curious than when they started, we have failed them.

The structure and type of learning that happens in many of our schools does not fulfill the needs of the twenty-first-century marketplace. When students graduate, many of them are good at one thing: school. They have mastered rubrics, they know how to ace tests, and they have figured out how to work within specific parameters. But the world is not a series of rubrics! To succeed, they will need to know how to think for themselves and adapt to constantly changing situations. And although we say we want kids to think for themselves, what we teach them is compliance. Seventeen-year-old Kate Simonds made this point in her 2015 TEDx Talk:

Look at our education system; as students, we have no
say on what we learn or how we learn it, yet we're expected to

absorb it all, take it all in, and be able to run the world some-
day. We're expected to raise our hands to use the restroom,
then three months later be ready to go to college or have a
full time job, support ourselves, and live on our own. It's not
logical.[2]

Compliance does not foster innovation. In fact, demanding conformity does quite the opposite.

In a world where new challenges constantly arise, students must be
taught to think critically about what they are facing. They must learn
to collaborate with others from around the world to develop solutions
for problems. Even more importantly, our students must learn how to
ask the right questions—questions that will challenge old systems and
inspire growth.

I'm not saying that today's schools are irrelevant *yet*. Many schools
and districts are not simply managing change, they are embracing it
and moving forward. What I *am* saying is that we need to change what
school looks like for our students so we can create new, relevant opportunities for them—for their future and for today.

First and foremost, if we want "innovative students," we will need
"innovative educators." Many of the rules of compliance that our students face in schools are the same ones educators face. Many teachers
are bored with the profession because they know there is a lot more to
learning than what schools offer today. These teachers want to be innovative, but, instead of connecting and learning from others around the
world, let alone with colleagues in their own schools, they spend their
time in staff meetings that often seem irrelevant to the heart of teaching. They are constantly told that if they want to be innovative, they are
going to have to find time to do it.

As leaders, if we ask teachers to use their own time to do anything,
what we're really telling them is: it's not important. The focus on compliance and implementation of programs in much of today's professional development does not inspire teachers to be creative , nor does
it foster a culture of innovation. Instead, it forces inspired educators

to color outside the lines, and even break the rules, to create relevant opportunities for their students. These outliers form pockets of innovation. Their results surprise us. Their students remember them as "great teachers," not because of the test scores they received but because their lives were touched.

These pockets of innovation have always existed in our schools; we need this to become the norm, not the exception. That means we must *make* time for our teachers to learn and grow. It also means that

IF STUDENTS LEAVE SCHOOL LESS CURIOUS THAN WHEN THEY STARTED, WE HAVE FAILED THEM.
#InnovatorsMindset

we need to develop a shared vision, align expectations, and provide pathways to ensure that all teachers have the resources to learn, create, and innovate to meet the needs of today's learners.

Building innovative organizations will take all of us working together. This is not about a "top down" or "bottom up" approach as much as it is about "all hands on deck." And it is possible.

An O2 commercial with the tagline "Be More Dog" illustrates how a decision can lead to extreme and positive changes. The ad shows the transformation of a lackadaisical cat who is bored with life until he decides to become "more dog."[3] (Take the time to watch the commercial, even if you are a cat lover . . . *especially* if you are a cat lover!) It focuses on taking risks, not avoiding but embracing change, and realizing that life is a much more enjoyable experience with an adventurous mindset.

Why would we *not* embrace the notion of "be more dog" in our schools?

The line from the video that resonates most with me is, "Look at the world today; it's amazing!" Think about it: we have the world at our fingertips, the ability to connect and create with people around the globe through so many different mediums. Yet what do most schools focus on when talking about technology? "Cyberbullying" and "digital safety." Yes, these are important concepts that should be discussed, but we need to go way beyond that. We are spending so much time telling our students about what they *can't do* that we have lost focus on what we *can do*. Imagine that if every time you talked about the ability to write with a pencil, you only focused on telling kids to not stab one another with the tool. What would you really inspire in your students? Creativity? Unlikely. Fear? Almost certainly.

This book is all about how we can make the most of learning to create meaningful change and provide better opportunities in our schools. The goal isn't to change for the sake of change but to make changes that allow us to empower our teachers and students to thrive. Here's a snapshot of what we'll cover.

In Part I, we will discuss what innovation is (and isn't) and what it means for schools. Additionally, we'll look at what it takes to develop an "innovator's mindset," its characteristics and what it looks like in practice.

In Part II, I will lay the groundwork for a culture of innovation in schools. We will begin with a focus on the importance of building solid relationships. As Stephen Covey states, nothing moves like the "speed of trust."[4] If we want people to take risks, they have to know we are there to catch them and support them. They also need to see us leading by example and taking risks in our work. Innovation is needed both in our classrooms and in our leadership. As leaders, we must model the kind of innovation we want to see.

The emphasis in this section is on moving away from a culture of compliance to create engagement and, ultimately, empower those in our schools. You'll learn that to truly empower people, there must be a shift from *telling* to *listening*. When you make that shift and focus on the learner (educator and student), rather than the administrator, you can create a shared vision for your community. When we tap into the power of *we* over *me*, we have the potential for what Steven Johnson refers to as the "adjacent possible," creating *new* aspirations and a powerful vision of what school could and should really be for our organization as learners. As Steven explains, the "adjacent possible" is not the endpoint, but the beginning:

> *The strange and beautiful truth about the adjacent possible is that its boundaries grow as you explore them. Each new combination opens up the possibility of other new combinations. Think of it as a house that magically expands with each door you open. You begin in a room with four doors, each leading to a new room that you haven't visited yet. Once you open one of those doors and stroll into that room, three new doors appear, each leading to a brand-new room that you couldn't have reached from your original starting point. Keep opening new doors and eventually you'll have built a palace.*[5]

Note: My intention with this book is not to tell you what your vision for education should be. Rather, my hope is that you will work with your community to understand and meet their unique needs, while embracing the opportunities for teaching and learning that are at your fingertips. It's about innovating within your school or organization—something no one knows better than you and your community.

Part III of this book is about action. The question I am most frequently asked in my talks and workshops is, "How do we get others to change?" In reality, you can't make anyone change; people can only change themselves. What you can do is create the conditions where change is more likely to happen. As a leader, you can create those conditions by taking a strengths-based approach for learning and leadership and unleashing talent in your organization. This section will also focus on harnessing the power of technology while ensuring that our decisions are led by learning. Additionally, we'll look at how you can create a culture that encourages everyone to be a teacher and a learner.

In Part IV, you'll define where you are, where you need to go, and how to get there. By the way, you will never "arrive." Leaders of the most innovative organizations in the world know there is no end to growth and learning. Schools, more than any other organization, need to embrace a commitment to continuous learning.

As you work through this book and implement changes, I hope you'll share your story because our students benefit when we learn from one another. I believe we can each make an impact—globally and locally—when we stop worrying about who is best and concern ourselves with helping *everyone* succeed. So don't hold back; share what you're learning and what's working for you.

Speaking of success, if you are looking for answers to create higher test scores, you might want to stop reading this book. Although I understand that we still work within a system, that's not what I choose to focus on. I believe it's possible to have kids who are deep thinkers, creators, and innovators, *and* still do well on their exams, but I do not want to forsake those critical elements for the latter. Twenty-first-century education is not about the test; it's about something bigger.

INNOVATION IS NOT RESERVED FOR THE FEW; IT IS SOMETHING WE WILL ALL NEED TO EMBRACE IF WE ARE TO MOVE FORWARD.

My focus is not on whether kids can knock it out of the park on some science test in grade three. What I care about is that kids are inspired to be better people because of their experiences in my school.

If you want to help others and make an impact on what school looks like for students and teachers, I hope this book will put you on that path. Creating change at the organizational level is something that our entire community—administrators, teachers, and especially students—should be part of. Innovation is not reserved for the few; it is something we will all need to embrace if we are to move forward.

When I think about my dad's life and how my mom continues to inspire me, I remember two lessons they taught me that will stick with me until the day I die. The first one is that relationships are at the crux of everything we do. They built a restaurant where people wanted to come and felt valued; they wouldn't have had a business, otherwise. In the same way, we need to, as *Teach Like a PIRATE* author Dave Burgess says, create an experience where students are "knocking down the doors to get in."[6] My hope is that this same enthusiasm will be felt by you and your staff. The second thing my parents taught me was the value of being a constant learner, especially in the face of adversity. If we can create school cultures in which values such as originality, creativity, critical thinking, collaboration, and an unquenchable thirst for knowledge are the norm of our students, our teachers, and ourselves, other organizations will look to education as an industry that leads in innovation, rather than one that is trying to catch up to the rest of the world.

Change can be hard and sometimes seemingly insurmountable, but remember, *change is an opportunity to do something amazing.* If we embrace this mindset and become the innovators our kids need (and need to be), the opportunities in front of us are endless.

Let's get started.

CONNECT. LEARN. INNOVATE. *SHARE.*
#InnovatorsMindset

Visit GeorgeCouros.ca or scan the
QR Code for additional resources.

NOTES

1. Dan Brown, "An Open Letter To Educators," YouTube video, 6:28, February 22, 2010, https://www.youtube.com/watch?v=-P2PGGeTOA4.

2. Kate Simonds, "I'm Seventeen," TEDx video, 13:39, February 10, 2015, http://tedxtalks.ted.com/video/I-m-Seventeen-%7C-Kate-Simonds-%7C;TEDxBoise.

3. 02, "Be More Dog," YouTube video, 1:10, July 4, 2013, https://www.youtube.com/watch?v=iMzgl0nFj3s.

4. Stephen M. R. Covey, *The Speed of Trust: The One Thing That Changes Everything* (New York: Free Press, 2006).

5. Steven Johnson, *Where Good Ideas Come From: The Natural History of Innovation* (New York: Riverhead Books, 2010).

6. Dave Burgess, *Teach Like a PIRATE: Increase Student Engagement, Boost Your Creativity, and Transform Your Life as an Educator* (San Diego: Dave Burgess Consulting, 2012).

PART I: INNOVATION IN EDUCATION

In the first part of this book, we will focus on defining innovation, looking at both what it is and what it isn't. Building on the understanding of innovation and why it's critical in education today, we will focus on the characteristics of the Innovator's Mindset. Examples will be shared, not with the intent to dictate what schools and educators should do, but to provoke thought and inspire you to create your own innovative approach in your practice as an individual and for your organization. There is an opportunity and necessity to create something new and better for our learners, both students and educators. For this to happen, the word "innovation" must be more than a buzzword in education—we will have to know what it is, what defines it, and what it looks like in practice.

CHAPTER 1
WHAT INNOVATION IS AND ISN'T

Change almost never fails because it's too early. It almost always fails because it's too late.

—Seth Godin[1]

I n an effort to bring the past alive, a historic tour of a Blockbuster store offers visitors a glimpse into the hardships of people who lived in the era of video stores. In a revealing video, reporters from *The Onion* interview period actors who explain that people once traveled great distances (sometimes six miles each way!) to rent and return movies. These poor souls lived in terror of never knowing if the movie they wanted would even be available![2]

The Onion's video, of course, is a satirical look at a company that tried to continue operating as if the Internet didn't exist. It was only a few years ago that video rental stores like Blockbuster were the best way for people to watch movies in the comfort of their own home. In some places around the world, these stores still exist. But in the Western world, cheaper and more convenient options (no travel required) have put most neighborhood video stores out of business.

The Internet completely changed the movie rental industry. Companies that took advantage of new technology, like Netflix with its DVD-by-mail and online streaming options, are thriving. Meanwhile, companies, like Blockbuster, that refuse to let go of outdated business models experience a slow, painful death.

Blockbuster had the opportunity to buy Netflix a few times, but declined.[3] And by the time it attempted to start its own DVD-by-mail program, the company had lost its place as an industry leader. The hard lesson that Blockbuster and its fellow neighborhood movie rental businesses failed to heed is this: innovate or die.

Savvy leaders understand the need for innovation and, as a result, constantly reinvent their organizations. Starbucks, for example, started off as a business that focused solely on selling coffee beans. Today, it is the best-known "coffee shop" in the world. Howard Schultz, the company's chairman and CEO, saw an opportunity to create a place where people would spend time away from home and work. Since its early days as a coffee bean roaster, the company's leaders have continually sought to improve the business—they find new ways to brew its coffees, including using high-tech machines that "control brew time and temperature digitally, using cloud technology to update recipes, track customer preferences and monitor coffee makers' performance."[4] They expanded the product line and now serve coffees and teas in a variety of forms and flavors. Starbucks is also known for its dedication to improving the way it serves its employees by offering life-friendly work schedules[5] and helping pay for employees to receive a university degree.[6]

Whether or not you like Starbucks coffee, the company is an example of an organization that is committed to constant improvement and adaptation to meet consumer demands. For Starbucks, change is about more than coffee or even survival; it's about success.

NEW OPPORTUNITIES

Learning and innovation go hand in hand. The arrogance of success is to think that what you did yesterday will be sufficient for tomorrow.

–William Pollard[1]

A common saying in education circles is, "We need to prepare kids for jobs that don't yet exist." In 2011, with that goal in mind, my superintendent, Tim Monds, and I created a job title: *Division Principal of Innovative Teaching and Learning*. It was a position that didn't exist in our district (or any other district we knew of at the time). We did not want to re-title an existing position and end up doing the same old things; we needed something new, something completely different. Tim and I, and other members of the district's leadership team, knew that a gap existed between what we were doing and what we needed to do. We also knew that if we were going to bridge that gap and create the kind of innovative organization we dreamed of, we needed to think differently.

I took on this position knowing that it was a bit of a risk. The risk came from the fact that there were no specific job requirements, only the expectation to help the district move forward. We were "building the plane in the air," and there was a chance I might crash and burn. Thankfully, my superintendent understood that the administration would have to take some risks, like devoting a person and funds to this task of innovative teaching and learning, if they wanted the rest of the leadership team to follow suit.

One of my first jobs in this position was to actually understand what *innovation* meant for our school district in the context of teaching and learning. We couldn't have *innovative teaching* and *learning* without first defining what that meant and how it could look for our teachers and students. This is not to say there were not innovative educators in our school district before this position was created. In fact, I knew quite a number of educators both inside and outside of our school district who were (and are) *extremely* forward-thinking in their approach to teaching and learning. But that innovation happened in pockets, and we wanted innovative teaching and learning to become the cultural norm in our school district.

HAVE SCHOOLS FORGOTTEN THEIR *WHY*?

Sometimes it scares me to think that we have taken the most human profession, teaching, and have reduced it to simply letters and numbers. We place such an emphasis on these scores, because of political mandates and the way teachers and schools are evaluated today, that it seems we've forgotten why our profession exists: to change—*improve*—lives. But, as speaker and author Dr. Joe Martin says so well, "No teacher has *ever* had a former student return to say a standardized test changed his or her life."

Shortly after I took on the position of Division Principal of Innovative Teaching and Learning, I watched a TED Talk by Simon Sinek, author of the best-selling book *Start with Why*. In his presentation, "How Great Leaders Inspire Action,"[8] he explained that all great organizations start with their "why" and *then* move toward the *what* and the *how*.

I believe education's *why* is to develop learners and leaders who will create a better present and future. When I use the term *leaders*, I'm not talking about *bosses* but people who have influence over and can make an impact on the world. Likewise, the term *learner* is not limited to students; educators must have the opportunity to develop both as learners and leaders. *Anyone* in any job or position—students, teachers, and administrators— can be a learner and a leader. But to develop these traits in our people, we must empower them; we must inspire innovation, rather than demand compliance.

My focus, and the *why* of this book, is developing schools that help individuals embrace the innovator's mindset. **When forward-thinking schools encourage today's learners to become creators and leaders, I believe they, in turn, will create a better world.** That's my why, and it's the way, I believe, we must approach the *what* and the *how* of our work as educators.

DEFINING INNOVATION

Innovation is a common term in many educational circles today and has been used a number of times in this book already. But what does it actually mean—especially in the terms of education?

For the purpose of this book, I'm defining innovation as a way of thinking that creates something *new* and *better.* Innovation can come from either "invention" (something totally new) or "iteration" (a change of something that already exists), but if it does not meet the idea of "new *and* better," it is not innovative. That means that change for the sake of change is never good enough. Neither is using *innovation* as a buzzword, as many organizations do, to appear current or relevant.

Note, too, that I said innovation is *a way of thinking.* It is a way of considering concepts, processes, and potential outcomes; it is not a thing, task, or even technology. As Carl Bass, CEO of Autodesk, explains in his TEDx talk "The New Rules of Innovation," "Innovation is the process by which we change the world.... It's the practical application of ideas and technologies to make new and better things."[9] So although many organizations approach innovation as if the word is synonymous with *technology*, it isn't. Technology can be crucial in the development of innovative organizations, but innovation is less about tools like computers, tablets, social media, and the Internet, and more about *how* we use those things.

Another word that is often used interchangeably with innovation is *transformation*, which is really more about dramatically altering the work educators do. Although I can see why some administrators are calling for transformation, the truth is innovation—in our thinking as individuals and organizations—is within easy reach; no dramatic shifts required. Katie Martin, director of professional learning at the University of San Diego Mobile Technology Learning Center, eloquently explains the importance of leadership in developing an innovative mindset:

> *There is no substitute for a teacher who designs authentic, participatory, and relevant learning experiences for her unique population of students. The role of the teacher is to inspire learning and develop skills and mindsets of learners. A teacher, as designer and facilitator, should continually evolve with resources, experiences, and the support of a community. It is becoming increasingly clear that we don't necessarily need to transform the role of teachers, rather create a culture that inspires and empowers teachers to innovate in the pursuit of providing optimal learning experiences for their students.[10]*

Establishing an innovative culture doesn't require transformation. However, it does require leaders who will develop and sustain systems that support "optimal learning experiences" and who value the process of creating and refining ideas.

INNOVATION STARTS WITH A QUESTION

According to Chicago-area teacher Josh Stumpenhorst, "Innovative teaching is constant evolution to make things better for student learning." Josh suggests that it is not teachers who are at the center of the classroom, but students—not as a whole, but as individuals. To create this type of environment, the question that must be asked every day is, "What is best for *this* learner?" Individualizing education and starting with empathy for those we serve is where innovative teaching and learning begins.

As we consider what's best for each learner, we must also think about how what we're teaching will impact his or her future. For example, one question I have asked many educators is, "In our world today, what is a student more likely going to need to be able to write: an essay or a blog post?" This question pushes some people to a place of discomfort (which is the point), but it also makes them think about what's relevant to today's educational needs. It isn't an either/or question. It is a question designed to make us think about why we do what we do. We need to ask more questions to provoke this type of thinking in education.

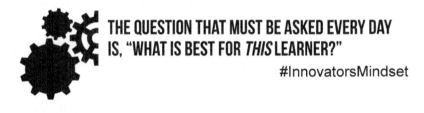

THE QUESTION THAT MUST BE ASKED EVERY DAY IS, "WHAT IS BEST FOR *THIS* LEARNER?"

#InnovatorsMindset

Any time teachers think differently about *who* they teach and *how* they teach, they can create better learning opportunities. Questioning what we do and *why* we do it is essential for innovation. For example, an English teacher might consider whether knowing how to embed a video is as important to communication as knowing how to cite an author or resource. For that matter, he or she may question which is more valuable to students: knowing how to embed a video or knowing how to create one? Of course, the answer to those questions depends on the context. The point is that questions like these make educators think differently; they force us to look at education from the perspective of the students' individual needs, as opposed to teaching content with which we are familiar and comfortable. Perhaps the components of writing an essay are crucial elements to writing an effective blog post. Thinking about how, what, and why we teach a lesson or skill helps ensure that we provide rich learning opportunities for our students.

OPEN INNOVATIVE LEARNING

One of my favorite people in the world, and a remarkable educator, is Bill Ferriter (@PlugUsIn) from Raleigh, North Carolina. Not only does he constantly push the boundaries of education within his own classroom, he also challenges other educators to stretch their thinking. Bill freely shares his creative presentations on his Flickr page. He's given his content a "Creative Commons" license, so others can modify them, with attribution to his original work. One of his pieces of work, a graphic titled, "What Do You Want Kids to Do with Technology?" caught my attention.[11] [See Figure 1.]

I shared his work and "remixed" it when I wrote a blog titled "What Do You Want Leaders to Do with Technology?"[12] Bill then took my ideas and created a new slide. [See Figure 2.]

In this simple example, you see an invention (Bill's original idea) and an iteration (my adaptation of his idea), both of which were designed with the intent of creating something new and better. Innovation is not always a "physical" creation. Many times, it is simply an idea. In this case, the graphics aren't the innovation—the *ideas* and the way they are applied are what hold the potential for innovative thinking. What is innovative about the graphics is the ability to freely

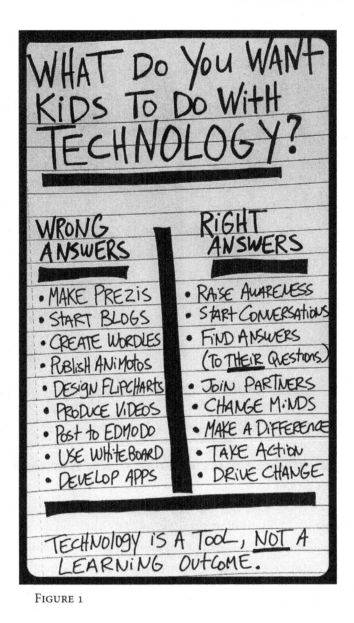

FIGURE 1

share and remix ideas for everyone's benefit—something that will be discussed at length in Chapter 11, "Embracing an Open Culture."

I wanted to use this example to point out innovation is not "new." In the past, innovative educators, like Bill Ferriter, who had excellent

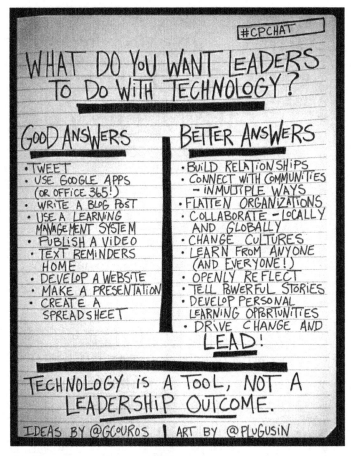

FIGURE 2

ideas also had limited opportunities to share their ideas. They might get a few minutes to share their thoughts at an occasional staff learning day. Today's technology makes it easy to quickly spread innovative ideas around the world. Bill's graphic, for example, has been viewed more than 43,000 times on Flickr at the time of this writing. Imagine how long it would have taken him to share his thoughts with that many people one-to-one or even in staff meetings. Technology has blown the roof off those old limitations.

SIMPLE STEPS TO INNOVATION

Sometimes a single idea can completely change our thinking. I remember talking to a grade one teacher about what she was teaching in her classroom. She told me her students were documenting plant growth by writing in their journals and drawing pictures of a plant as it grew. Each week she responded to the students individually about their projects. We talked about her goals for the class and, together, came up with an innovative idea that accomplished several things. The teacher created an Instagram account (instagram.com/pvsgreen-thumbs) for the class. Students took and posted pictures and documented what they saw in the caption box. Putting the project online meant that the teacher, parents, as well as people around the world could comment on the students' posts. With this one adaptation to her lesson, the teacher had successfully crowdsourced learning. And although the main objective was to focus on plant growth, these six- and seven-year-old students also learned about their digital footprint and about what to post—and what not to post—online.

Simply put, the project was a new and better way of teaching and learning. The opportunity to learn from people outside their classroom and to bring parents into the conversation (which also improved the

WHEN WE THINK DIFFERENTLY ABOUT THE THINGS THAT WE ARE USED TO SEEING DAILY, WE CAN CREATE INNOVATIVE LEARNING OPPORTUNITIES.

learning that went on at home) came from a simple shift in mindset. Was it a life-changing event? No, but it was a step in the right direction. And it proves the point that, when we think differently about the things that we are used to seeing daily, we can create innovative learning opportunities—for our teachers and students.

WHAT INNOVATION ISN'T

The "Think Different" idea that Apple is famously known for is a good start, but *different* isn't enough to make something innovative or beneficial. For example, many schools today have replaced unhealthy "junk" food in their vending machines with healthier items. The thinking is that providing healthy snacks leaves students with no option but to make better food choices. The tactic is intended to encourage better eating habits, and that's a worthy goal. But in many schools, this approach has failed. Instead of eating what's available at school, some students go to nearby convenience stores and buy unhealthy food in larger portions. In this case, different isn't proving to be better for our students, who end up spending more and eating worse.

The voice that has often been missing in these health initiatives is that of the students. To help people change, it is important to understand what drives their habits in the first place.

Different for the sake of different can be a waste of time and may even leave us worse off than where we started. Simply replacing "A" with "B" is not only *not* innovation but it could actually lead to something worse than what we had before. Designing solutions with both the individuals' interests and the end goal in mind is crucial for any innovation to be successful.

MOVING FORWARD

One of John Maxwell's famous quotes is, "Change is inevitable. Growth is optional."[13] In many respects, that sentiment is true. We choose whether or not we will grow, change, or innovate. But in schools, where we focus on our students as the future, growth can no longer be simply an *option*.

Change is constant, and I stated earlier that change is an opportunity to do something amazing. Perhaps the *amazing* thing we can do is make growth mandatory—for ourselves as educators, as well as for our students. That is how we can truly serve our children.

Education cannot become the new Blockbuster where we refused to embrace the new in hopes that the old ways will suffice. In a world that constantly changes, if our focus is to only maintain what's already been done, we are bound to become worse. The innovator's mindset is necessary for all of us if schools are to move forward.

QUESTIONS FOR DISCUSSION

1. What is an example of a practice that you consider to be innovative? How is it new or better than what you had before?

2. How can you create opportunities for innovation in your leadership? In your teaching? In your learning?

3. What has changed in our world today that not only makes innovation easier to do, but is also necessary for our students?

NOTES

1. Seth Godin, *Tribes: We Need You to Lead Us* (New York: Portfolio, 2008), 101.

2. The Onion, "Historic 'Blockbuster' Store Offers Glimpse of How Movies Were Rented in The Past," *TheOnion.com* video, 2:07, May 12, 2008, http://www.theonion.com/video/historic-blockbuster-store-offers-glimpse-of-how-m-14233.

3. Marc Graser, "Epic Fail: How Blockbuster Could Have Owned Netflix," *Variety*, November 12, 2013, http://variety.com/2013/biz/news/epic-fail-how-blockbuster-could-have-owned-netflix-1200823443/.

4. Kate Taylor, "3 Ways Starbucks Is Innovating and Why You Should Care," *Entrepreneur*, October 23, 2013, http://www.entrepreneur.com/article/229580.

5. Khushbu Shah, "Starbucks to Improve Its Employees Schedules," *Eater*, August 15, 2014, http://eater.com/archives/2014/08/15/starbucks-to-improve-its-employees-schedules.php.

6. Leslie Patton, "Starbucks to Pick up Tab for Employees' University Degrees," *Financial Post*, June 26, 2014, http://business.financialpost.com/2014/06/16/starbucks-to-pick-up-tab-for-employees-university-degrees/.

7. C. William Pollard, *The Soul of the Firm* (Grand Rapids, MI: Zondervan, 1996), 114.

8. Simon Sinek, "How Great Leaders Inspire Action," TED Talk video, 18:04, September 2009, http://www.ted.com/talks/simon_sinek_how_great_leaders_inspire_action?language=en.

9. Carl Bass, "The New Rules of Innovation," YouTube video, 17:33, February 25, 2012, https://www.youtube.com/watch?v=YKV3rhzvaC8.

10. Katie Martin, "Creating a Culture of Innovation Versus Transformation," *katielmartin.com*, June 10, 2015, http://katielmartin. com/2015/06/10/creating-a-culture-of-innovation-vs-a-transformation/.

11. Images used with permission: Bill Ferriter, @PlugUsIn, http:// blog.williamferriter.com.

12. George Couros, "What Do You Want Leaders to Do with Technology?", *The Principal of Change: Stories of Leading and Learning*, February 4, 2015, http://georgecouros.ca/blog/archives/5056.

13. John C. Maxwell, *A Leader's Heart: 365-Day Devotional Journal* (Nashville, Thomas Nelson, 2003), 54.

CHAPTER 2
THE INNOVATOR'S MINDSET

We need to move beyond the idea that an education is something that is provided for us and toward the idea that an education is something that we create for ourselves.

—Stephen Downes (2010)[1]

In a powerful scene from the television reality series *Educating Yorkshire,*[2] a teacher working with a student who has a stammer tries a technique he saw in *The King's Speech.* In the movie, King George VI (played by Colin Firth) used music to help ease his stammer. The teacher suggests that his student, Musharaf Asghar, listen to music while trying to read a poem aloud. It works! Both the teacher and student are amazed by the quick results. Later, Asghar, who is described as a student who had been bullied and wanted to leave school because he "didn't have a voice," reads a speech to his entire class. His fellow students and teachers are blown away and visibly moved by his ability to speak. Teachers are crying. Students are crying. Mr. Burton, the teacher who cared so much about his students that he was willing to try something new and provide a different path to success, beams with pride as the assembly erupts with applause.

Overcoming his stammer gave Musharaf a profound sense of confidence—and the opportunity to host a documentary about stuttering and speech therapy.[3] And it happened because his teacher embraced the *innovator's mindset*.

ADOPT AN INNOVATOR'S MINDSET

Carol Dweck, a Stanford psychologist and author of the powerful book *Mindset: The New Psychology of Success*, encourages educators to introduce students to the concept of a growth mindset. She explains

 THE ABILITY TO INNOVATE—TO CREATE SOMETHING NEW AND BETTER—IS A SKILL THAT ORGANIZATIONS WORLDWIDE ARE LOOKING FOR TODAY. #InnovatorsMindset

that teaching children the difference between a "fixed" and "growth" mindset empowers them. They learn that trying new things, even if they initially fail, stretches and strengthens their minds.

In a fixed mindset, students believe their basic abilities, their intelligence, their talents, are just fixed traits. They have a certain amount and that's that, and then their goal becomes to look smart all the time and never look dumb. In a growth mindset, students understand that their talents and abilities can be developed through effort, good teaching, and persistence. They don't necessarily think everyone's the same or anyone can be Einstein, but they believe everyone can get smarter if they work at it.[4]

FIXED MINDSET

GROWTH MINDSET

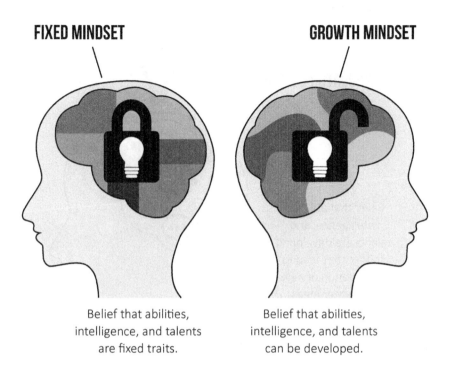

Belief that abilities, intelligence, and talents are fixed traits.

Belief that abilities, intelligence, and talents can be developed.

Let's take the simple example of playing the piano to compare the two ideas. With a *fixed mindset*, the learner doesn't believe he or she has the ability to play the piano. With a *growth mindset*, the learner believes that, with hard work and practice, the opportunity to play the piano is within the realm of his or her ability. That belief leads the learner to *try* and, ultimately, grow.[5]

The *innovator's mindset* takes the growth mindset a step further by focusing on using one's ability to learn to play the piano to *create* music. The innovator's mindset can be defined as *the belief that the abilities, intelligence, and talents are developed so that they lead to the creation of new and better ideas.*

The growth mindset is crucial in one's openness to learning. But to change education and prepare students for their futures, we need to adopt an innovator's mindset for ourselves and instill this mindset in our students. We must focus on *creating* something with the knowledge that's been acquired.[6]

THE INNOVATOR'S MINDSET

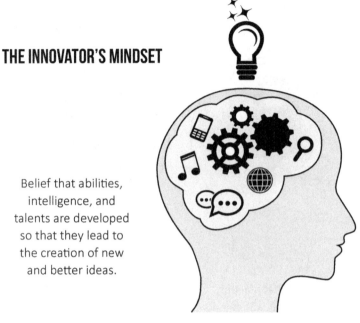

Belief that abilities, intelligence, and talents are developed so that they lead to the creation of new and better ideas.

The ability to innovate—to create something new and better—is a skill that organizations worldwide are looking for today. Thomas Friedman notes in his *New York Times* piece, "How to Get a Job at Google," that translating knowledge into action is perhaps even more important than acquiring information.

> *Google attracts so much talent it can afford to look beyond traditional metrics, like G.P.A. For most young people, though, going to college and doing well is still the best way to master the tools needed for many careers... Beware. Your degree is not a proxy for your ability to do any job.* **The world only cares about—and pays off on—what you can do with what you know (and it doesn't care how you learned it).**[7]

Let's go back to the example of the young man with the stammer. The teacher watched *The King's Speech* and used what he learned (not from a university class, professional learning day, or any other type of formal learning opportunity) to create a new opportunity for his student. Although they used technology (a smart phone and head-phones), it was very simple. Listening to music through a personal device is something we've done since the invention of the Walkman in 1979. The technology was not innovative, but the use of it was.

Learning to recognize and create new and better opportunities for our students is what matters. In fact, it's essential.

SHOULD EVERY EDUCATOR HAVE AN INNOVATOR'S MINDSET?

The short answer to the question above is *yes*.

Why? Because all teachers have worked with students who couldn't seem to "get" the lesson or master a new skill despite numerous attempts and various teaching methods. When the approaches you've used with other students don't work, do you give up on the struggling student? No! At least, I hope not. My hope is that you'll see the challenge as an

 INNOVATION IS NOT ABOUT THE *STUFF*, IT IS A WAY OF THINKING.
#InnovatorsMindset

opportunity to take what you know, find out what you need to know, and try to figure out a new way to teach the material or skill—one that works for that specific student.

Similarly, almost all administrators face budget constraints and work within a system that expects more and better results with less funding. Thankfully, innovation is not about the *stuff*; it is a way of thinking. Our challenge as leaders is to think of new ways to do things so we can move forward. We live in a complex world that needs us to look for new and better ways to solve problems and help those we serve.

INNOVATION INSIDE THE BOX

Brad Gustafson (@gustafsonbrad), a forward-thinking principal in Minnesota, is a prime example of a leader who successfully works within those budget constraints. I distinctly remember being on a panel at the Michigan Association for Computer Users in Learning (MACUL) conference with Brad as he talked about some of the amazing initiatives and innovation in his school. Someone in the audience asked, "Where do you find the money to do this?"

His answer was both simple and brilliant: "We made a budget line titled 'innovation,' and we moved money from one spot to another." Brad didn't look to some outside source for money that would enable his school to focus on innovative ideas. He took what he had and used it to meet the needs of his school.

Let's not kid ourselves. In education, especially the public sector, schools are not overloaded with funding. Innovating in our schools requires a different type of thinking, one that doesn't focus on ideas that are "outside of the box" but those that allow us to be innovative despite budgetary constraints. In other words, we need to learn to innovate inside the box. Like Brad, we need to look at the realities of our situations and create something new. And it's crucial that educators see this "inside the box innovation" modeled by administrators.

WHAT PART OF FAILURE DO WE EMBRACE?

A mantra that's often repeated when we talk about innovation in education is that *failure is an important part of the process.* In some respects, it's true. Unfortunately, this line of thinking can place a focus on the wrong aspect of the process. Those who stress the importance of failure as part of the innovation process tend to focus on failure. They'll point to stories about inventors like James Dyson, the inventor of the

Dyson vacuum. Dyson "spent fifteen years creating 5,126 versions that failed before he made one that worked."[8] Trying, failing, and trying again were definitely part of his process. But the reality of his story is that no one would even mention James Dyson if he hadn't succeeded in the end. How many other vacuum inventors can you name? Maybe one or two. But how many vacuum inventors can you name who never successfully got a vacuum on the market? *Zero.*

Having the freedom to fail *is* important to innovation. But even more important to the process are the traits of *resiliency* and *grit.* *Resiliency* is the ability to come back after a defeat or unsuccessful attempt. *Grit* is resolve or strength of character. These two characteristics need to be continuously developed as we look for new and better ways to serve our students.

For example, I was recently talking to a learning coach who shared her frustration about working with another teacher who basically tried one process with a student. The process didn't work, and when her

> HAVING THE FREEDOM TO FAIL IS IMPORTANT TO INNOVATION. BUT EVEN MORE IMPORTANT TO THE PROCESS ARE THE TRAITS OF RESILIENCY AND GRIT.

learning coach asked her whether she tried anything else, the teacher had admitted she hadn't. The learning coach was obviously frustrated that this was a "one and done" situation. Later, our group conversation turned to focus on the notion of failure and how it is important that educators "embrace" and be okay with it. I immediately jumped in and asked the learning coach, "Do you consider the process you described earlier as a failure?" When she replied, "Yes," I asked, "Were you okay with that?"

"NO!" she emphatically replied.

And that's the point. Trying different things and figuring out alternative options for our students are all part of the innovator's mindset. But accepting failure as a final outcome, especially when it comes to our kids, is not something we should ever embrace.

When I first started teaching, I remember thinking that students should learn the way I taught; they should adjust to me. I could not have been more wrong. A great teacher adjusts to the learner, not the other way around. This is where *resiliency* and *grit* are necessary. Understanding failure happens but also not accepting failure as a result is paramount in serving our students. What works for one might not work for another. As leaders, we need to develop a culture that focuses on doing whatever it takes to ensure that we are successful in serving all of our students.

Imagine you took a large chunk of your money, gave it to an investor, they lost it all, and they said, "Failure is just part of the process." Although there might be some truth to that statement, it still probably wouldn't sit well with you. When it comes to our kids, we have a lot more to lose than money. Go back to the teacher and the student with the stammer. Part of Mr. Burton's mindset was that he was open to trying something that might

INNOVATION STARTS NOT BY PROVIDING ANSWERS BUT BY ASKING QUESTIONS.

#InnovatorsMindset

not work. What he cared about *most* was finding something that *would* work—a technique that empowered his student to succeed. That is the innovator's mindset exemplified: Try, fail, and try something else until you find or create a solution that works.

Innovation, though, starts not by providing answers but by asking questions. To be innovative, these questions focus on having empathy for those we serve. What is often misunderstood is that the higher up any one person is in any organization, the more people they serve, not the other way around. In education, as in any other organization, to be truly innovative, the process will be driven by asking questions, as each community and individual we serve is unique. The questions below mean to provide a starting point.

CRITICAL QUESTIONS FOR THE INNOVATIVE EDUCATOR

Would I want to be a learner in my own classroom?

In my experience creating professional learning opportunities, I've found that it can be challenging to meet the needs and expectations of educators. They have high expectations for their own learning experiences, not only because they are expected to create those same environments for their own classrooms but also because their time is limited. Educators rarely have enough time to take care of their myriad of responsibilities. If professional learning doesn't provide relevant experiences and skills to help them make a greater impact on the students they serve, many educators will disengage.

For example, if worksheets were handed out as professional learning, some teachers would be bored to tears, yet, in many cases, we do the same thing to our students. That type of learning is not about what is better for kids but what is easy or because it's the way it has always been done. Consider your students' learning experience from their point of view. Do your students have opportunities to learn in ways that connect to their lives and make an impact on how they engage with the others? Do the learning experiences you create mimic the type of learning you expect to engage in? Think about the classroom experience from your students' perspective; establish a higher expectation for learning opportunities.

What is best for **this** *student?*

It is important to not only think about the perspective of your class as a whole but to also know each student and what works for him or her. Because each individual learns differently, it's important to ask, "How does this student learn best?" and "What are some ways students can demonstrate their knowledge?" For example, for students who are trying to share their understanding of any curriculum objective, is writing it down every time the only way they can show what they understand? Could they create a video, share a podcast, create a visual, or do something else?

What is this student's passion?

When I was in school, I remember being required to read novel after novel, even though I was not interested in the assigned books. I was never once asked to read non-fiction in school, even though that is what interested me most. It was nearly impossible to get me to read a novel, but, at any point in a day, I would head off to the library and read every *Sports Illustrated* that I could get my hands on. That passion could and *should* have been tapped into in my school experience.

One of the best experiences I have ever had as an educator was "Identity Day." On that day, the kids shared about the things they loved outside of school in a type of display or presentation. There was such an enthusiasm to share their interests. As educators, we can create better experiences for our students by tapping into their passions. To do so, we need to be intentional about learning more about our students and what they love.

What are some ways we can create a true learning community?

I remember hearing someone once ask, "Why is it that when kids leave school, they have a ton of energy and teachers are tired? Why isn't it the other way around?" The reality is that the experiences we create often make students dependent upon the teacher for learning. What would be beneficial for our students and ourselves is to have them tap into one another's expertise, not just the teacher's knowledge. Things such as blogging, Edmodo, Google apps, and using Twitter hashtags in the classroom provide opportunities for our students to learn from each other. By embracing the idea that *everyone* in the classroom is a teacher and a learner, we can create a community that learns from and teaches one another.

How did this work for our students?

Early in my teaching career, I always asked for feedback from my students at the end of the year. Doing so helped me improve my teaching for the next set of students, but that feedback did nothing to help the kids who had been in my classroom that year. A better approach is to get feedback throughout the year, not just in the form of grades but through conversations. Additionally, allowing for anonymous comments ensures that students feel comfortable sharing their thoughts. Regular feedback helps us reflect on how we are serving our current students.

MOVING FORWARD

Success for our students—and for ourselves—isn't about how much we know, how efficient our systems are, or even the scores our students earn. It is, as Friedman wrote, about "what you can do with what you know." Information is abundant; it's common. What's uncommon, and desperately needed in today's education systems, is the *innovator's mindset*.

INFORMATION IS ABUNDANT; IT'S COMMON. WHAT'S UNCOMMON, AND DESPERATELY NEEDED IN TODAY'S EDUCATION SYSTEMS, IS THE INNOVATOR'S MINDSET.

The innovator's mindset starts with empathy for our students (which is why the questions above are so crucial). Equally important is the desire to create something better. If we are going to help our students thrive, we have to move past "the way we have always done it," and create better learning experiences for our students than we had ourselves. This does not mean replacing everything we do, but we must being willing to look with fresh eyes at what we do and ask, "Is there a better way?" We would expect the same mindset from our students, and, as educators, that question is the first step on the path to a better future for education.

QUESTIONS FOR DISCUSSION

1. What are some examples of innovation that you have seen within constraints, both inside and outside of schools?

2. What questions do you think are vital to understanding those who we serve in education?

3. If you were to start a school from scratch, what would it look like?

4. How do we take what we currently have to create a better education system for our entire community?

NOTES

1. Stephen Downes, "A World to Change," *The Huffington Post*, October 18, 2010, http://www.huffingtonpost.com/stephen-downes/a-world-to-change_b_762738.html.

2. *Educating Yorkshire,* BBC, Episode 8, October 24, 2013. http://www.channel4.com/programmes/educating-yorkshire/on-demand.

3. Maggie Brown, "Musharaf Asghar, Star of *Educating Yorkshire*, Gets a Show of His Own," *The Guardian*, August 16, 2014, http://gu.com/p/4vnq7/stw.

4. James Morehead, "Stanford University's Carol Dweck on the Growth Mindset and Education," *OneDublin.org*, June 19, 2012, http://onedublin.org/2012/06/19/stanford-universitys-carol-dweck-on-the-growth-mindset-and-education/.

5. George Couros, "The Innovator's Mindset," *The Principal of Change: Stories of Learning and Leading* (blog), September 11, 2014, http://georgecouros.ca/blog/archives/4728.

6. *Ibid.*

7. Thomas Friedman, "How to Get a Job at Google," *The New York Times*, February 22, 2014, http://www.nytimes.com/2014/02/23/opinion/sunday/friedman-how-to-get-a-job-at-google.html?_r=0.

8. Nadia Goodman, "James Dyson on Using Failure to Drive Success," *Entrepreneur*, November 4, 2012, http://www.entrepreneur.com/article/224855.

CHAPTER 3
CHARACTERISTICS OF THE INNOVATOR'S MINDSET

With continuous advances in technology and learning, a three-year absence from teaching could easily seem like thirty to an educator who is returning to the classroom. It's no surprise, then, that Lisa Jones, an accomplished high school teacher in Peel School district just outside of Toronto, Canada, felt as if she had fallen behind when she first came back to teaching after a three-year maternity leave. That feeling intensified when she pulled out the overhead projector.

Only a few years earlier, the overhead projector was considered to be a crucial technology in education. But as Lisa switched out the transparencies for her mitosis lesson, she suddenly realized how boring it was for her. The methods she had previously used to teach these concepts were not meeting the needs of her students today.

As Lisa shared her concern, it was obvious to me that she wanted to get better. She knew that, if she were a student, she would have hated the traditional mitosis lesson she had just delivered. She also knew she didn't want to limit her students' opportunities to the knowledge she had at the time—knowledge that hadn't yet caught up with the current technology available to her and her students. As we talked about her options, I asked her to consider going onto Twitter and connecting with other science educators using the hashtag #scichat. Since she was new to Twitter, I showed a video called "Twitter in 60 Seconds" to give her a quick, introductory explanation of how teachers can use Twitter.

A week later, Lisa sent me the following tweet: "@gcouros you inspired me to do this lesson—here is one of the products!"[1] She included a link to a student-produced YouTube video titled "Mitosis in 60 Seconds."

I was blown away by the progress Lisa made in such a short time. With a desire to create new and better learning experiences, and a model of a new way of learning, she took a risk to make that happen. After watching the "Twitter in 60 Seconds" video, Lisa showed it

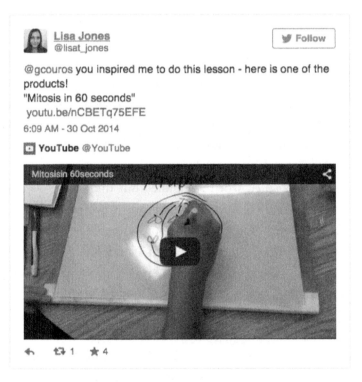

to her students and asked, "Could you do this for mitosis?" Although she wasn't confident she could create the video herself, Lisa knew her students would be able to figure out the technology—and maybe she could learn from *them*. Notice that Lisa still taught the mitosis content, but with an innovative and effective twist. In fact, she told me later that it was the first time every single student in her class passed the course.

Lisa's experience is one example that proves we do not have to sacrifice innovation because of expectations or limitations. This goes back to the idea of being innovative *inside of the box*—in this case, creating new and better methods to teach the required curriculum. My belief is that great educators can work within the constraints of the system and still create innovative learning opportunities for their students. In fact, I think it is necessary to do so.

I believe that the majority of educators *want* to create engaging and effective learning experiences for their students to achieve the desired learning goals. No teacher wakes up in the morning and says, "I can't wait to go to school and be mediocre!" I talk with teachers all the time and I know they desire to do great things for the students they serve. But at the same time, there are tremendous demands placed on teachers today and, too often, the narrative I hear from so many administrators is, "Teachers don't want to change!" My belief is not that teachers don't want to *change*, but they sometimes lack clear guidance and support to make the desired change. Effective leadership in education is not about moving everyone from one standardized point to the next but moving individuals from *their point "A" to their point "B."*

GREAT EDUCATORS CAN WORK WITHIN THE CONSTRAINTS OF THE SYSTEM AND STILL CREATE INNOVATIVE LEARNING OPPORTUNITIES FOR THEIR STUDENTS.

When we approach leadership with an innovator's mindset, we lead with empathy—meeting people where they are—to help them find or create solutions that work for them. If I, as an education and innovation coach, had told Lisa she'd better use technology or demanded to see specific grade outcomes for her course, she, like many teachers feel compelled to do, may have clung to what she knew and hoped for the best—even if that meant the lesson was boring and ineffective.

Empathizing with Lisa to understand her goals and providing both a model and encouragement empowered her to create a new learning experience—for her and her students.

THE 8 CHARACTERISTICS OF THE INNOVATOR'S MINDSET

I've identified eight crucial characteristics that are necessary for an innovator's mindset, not only for teachers but also for everyone involved in education.[2] As you read through them, consider how Lisa demonstrated each of these characteristics in her teaching. (Many thanks to Sylvia Duckworth, @sylviaduckworth, for her illustration of these characteristics.)[3]

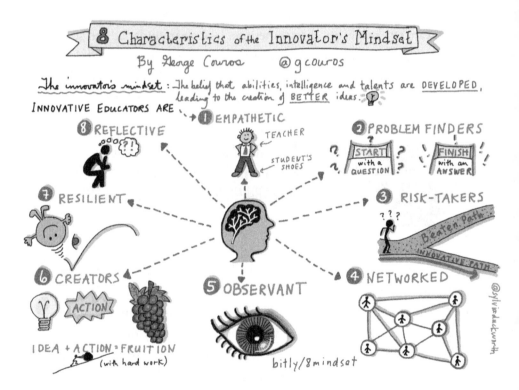

8 Characteristics of the Innovator's Mindset

By George Couros   @gcouros

The innovator's mindset: The belief that abilities, intelligence and talents are DEVELOPED, leading to the creation of BETTER ideas.

INNOVATIVE EDUCATORS ARE

1. EMPATHETIC — TEACHER — STUDENT'S SHOES
2. PROBLEM FINDERS — START with a QUESTION — FINISH with an ANSWER
3. RISK-TAKERS — Beaten Path — INNOVATIVE PATH
4. NETWORKED
5. OBSERVANT
6. CREATORS — ACTION — IDEA + ACTION = FRUITION (with hard work)
7. RESILIENT
8. REFLECTIVE

bitly/8mindset

1. **Empathetic**—In the previous chapter, I mentioned that educators have exceptionally high expectations for their own learning experiences because they focus on creating powerful learning opportunities for students every single day. High expectations are not bad, in fact, they can be used to our advantage. And it's why I regularly ask educators to consider the question: **Would you want to be a learner in your own classroom?**

   Empathetic teachers think about the classroom environment and learning opportunities from the point of view of the student, not the teacher. Lisa, for example, understood that the way she originally delivered the information did not allow for the students to interact with the content in a meaningful way. It was familiar and easy for her, but it didn't engage her learners' needs or appeal to their interests. To remedy that, Lisa flipped the classroom from being *teacher-centric* to *learner-centric*. She shifted her role and became the architect of the experience, while her students actually created the learning for themselves.

   Because of Lisa's willingness to develop relationships with her students, she understood them. She knew that at least some of them knew how to create media, and enjoyed doing so, but did not necessarily connect that process to what they did in school. By tapping into their interests, she crafted an innovative learning experience.

2. **Problem Finders/Solvers**—For years, schools have posed questions or *problems* to students, often in a linear model that forces students to follow certain steps to find the answer. The world is not step-by-step or linear; it's complex and often requires a messy solution. Sometimes it takes several attempts and iterations to solve real-life problems, and, sometimes, there are several correct answers. But solving a problem is only one part of learning. Educational thought leader Ewan McIntosh notes that *finding* the problem is an essential part of learning—one that students miss out on when we pose the problem to them first.

Currently the world's educational systems are crazy about problem-based learning, but they're obsessed with the wrong bit of it. While everyone looks at how we could help young people become better problem-solvers, we're not thinking how we could create a generation of problem finders.[4]

We see elements of problem finding in Lisa's approach. She felt her students were not experiencing deep learning, and she knew something was wrong, even though no one was challenging her to do anything different. Although she suggested the idea of creating a video, she also gave them the freedom to explore other options for sharing their learning in a compelling way. Additionally, she challenged her students to figure out how to create the presentation on their own.

Teaching students by example to be self-starters and to continuously evaluate how they might improve their education helps them *learn how to effectively learn*. When we stop simply telling students how to learn, and, rather, act as a "guide on the side," we can support them in a way that encourages them to find their own solutions.

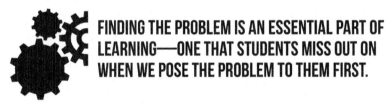

FINDING THE PROBLEM IS AN ESSENTIAL PART OF LEARNING—ONE THAT STUDENTS MISS OUT ON WHEN WE POSE THE PROBLEM TO THEM FIRST.

Sometimes teachers need to lead from the front. Other times, our students' learning experiences are improved when we move alongside them or simply get out of the way. The right approach is determined by understanding our students' needs at any given time—foundational to this is building relationships with the diverse learners in your classroom.

3. **Risk Takers**—Innovative teaching and learning involve taking risks. If we are to create new opportunities for the learners we serve, not everything we try will always work with every learner. If we're honest, we'll admit that's always been the case. Many of our known "best practices" don't serve a large number of our students. So why would we take risks in the classroom, especially when it may affect our students' futures? The answer lies in the question. Risk is necessary to ensure that we are meeting the needs of each unique student. Some respond well to one way of learning, while others need a different method or format. Not taking the risk to find the best approach for each student might seem less daunting than trying new things, but maintaining the status quo may have dire consequences for our students.

   When we think of risk, we shouldn't just challenge what *doesn't* work. It's also necessary to question our "best practices." Lisa could have continued using the overhead projector and transparencies, and some of her students would have done extremely well on any assessment given. But did they really gain deep knowledge about concepts and how to apply them? Or did they simply learn to regurgitate information? In many cases, we have conditioned kids to "schooling." Accustomed to and successful in controlled learning environments, some students may fear being educated (and assessed) in any other way. But they don't start out fearful. Think about how curious kindergarten students are and how many questions they ask when they first walk into school! I can guarantee that none of those little ones ask for a worksheet. We condition them to that. If we really want to serve our students and help them to develop into the leaders and learners of today and the future, taking risks in our practice is not only encouraged but necessary.

   An educator with an innovative mindset will find the balance between drawing on experience while maintaining a willingness to try something new. Apple started by making great computers, and computers are still a major part of its business. But the company's leaders went out on a limb to create the iPhone—a risk that led to one of Apple's biggest achievements. That "risk" also spawned other successful endeavors, including the App Store, iPad, and the Apple Watch. Likewise, for Lisa, the success her students experienced because of the risk she took has led to her implementing more innovative ideas. What is important is that she feels confident asking the question, "Is there a better way to teach this lesson to meet the needs of these learners?"

4. **Networked**—Networks are crucial to innovation. CIO.com writer Tom Kaneshige says, "Every idea is fundamentally a network of ideas... When you create an environment that allows the kinds of serendipitous connections to form, [innovative ideas] are more likely to happen."[5]

   Being in spaces where people actively share ideas makes us smarter. Think about all of the actors who flock to Hollywood, or all of the country singers who end up in Nashville, or all of the "startups" that are situated in Silicon Valley. In these networks where so many people with similar interests in an area gather, innovation occurs almost spontaneously.

   Face-to-face networking is still crucial and valuable in education, but, today, social media provides a place for ideas to spread. Steven Anderson, well-known educational speaker and writer says, "Alone we are smart, together we are brilliant." The power of networking is sharing ideas, clarifying our thinking, and developing new and better ideas.

   When students come to school, we continually tell them, "You need to share!" because we know the great benefit to their learning. Educators would all benefit if we decided to take our own advice. One way we can do that is through blogs. If you're thinking, "I'm not a writer," consider this: every opportunity to share with others on a global scale makes you think more deeply about what it is that you are sharing in the first place. In Clive

Thompson's *Wired* article "Why Even the Worst Bloggers Are Making Us Smarter," he explains how having an audience can enhance learning:

> *Having an audience can clarify thinking. It's easy to win an argument inside your head. But when you face a real audience, you have to be truly convincing.*
>
> *Social scientists have identified something called the audience effect—the shift in our performance when we know people are watching. It isn't always positive. In live, face-to-face situations, like sports or concerts, the audience effect can make athletes or musicians perform better—but it can sometimes psych them out and make them choke, too.*
>
> *Yet studies have found that the effort of communicating to someone else forces you to pay more attention and learn more.*[6]

Innovation (and enjoyment) flourishes when teachers collaborate to learn and practice new strategies. Isolation is often the enemy of innovation.

5. **Observant**—Let's go back to the example of Lisa and her students. Lisa first connected with other educators through social media. Specifically, she searched the hashtag #scichat to find other teachers on Twitter who were interested in the subject of science. Online she saw other teachers who pushed the expectations for what could be done by students. Yet her idea for having students create their own "Mitosis in 60 Seconds" videos didn't come from that network but from watching the "Twitter in 60 Seconds" video. The lesson? Sometimes, the most valuable thing you get from the network isn't an idea but the inspiration or courage to try something new.

Ideas for education today are *not* limited to education. Many educators have taken ideas from Google, FedEx, or from any number of YouTube videos, including TED Talks (TED is short for technology, entertainment, and design). Chris Anderson, the entrepreneur, journalist, and publisher who curates TED Talks, calls the effect of web videos on learning, "crowd-accelerated innovation"[7] (which will be discussed further in Chapter 11). Because of Chris's dedication to exposing others' brilliance to the entire world through online videos, millions of people have heard talks on edu-

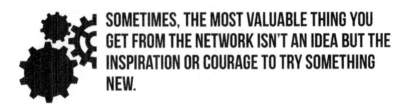 SOMETIMES, THE MOST VALUABLE THING YOU GET FROM THE NETWORK ISN'T AN IDEA BUT THE INSPIRATION OR COURAGE TO TRY SOMETHING NEW.

cation done by the likes of Sir Ken Robinson and Rita Pierson. And you are not limited to the minds of those focused solely on the field education. People from a variety of fields, such as Daniel Pink (speaking about motivation), Barry Schwartz (sharing his thoughts on wisdom), or Susan Cain (focusing on the power of introverts), have had a major impact on educators worldwide.

Making connections between the powerful ideas and information that's being freely shared online allows educators to expand learning possibilities for their students. Josh Stumpenhorst is one educator who has done exactly that. After watching Daniel Pink's TED Talk and reading more from him about the topics of motivation and the power of autonomy, Josh created an "Innovation Day" in which his students proposed and worked on their own ideas and inventions. The day was so successful that Josh's students were willing to come to school on a Saturday to continue the learning. If Josh had not been willing to learn from ideas being shared outside of education *and* connect those ideas to the needs of his students, he might not have created such a powerful learning opportunity.

My dream is that, by creating a culture of innovation in education and sharing our ideas with the world, organizations will look to schools for ideas to become innovative, not the other way around.

Inspiration is everywhere and often in unexpected places; you just have to keep your eyes open.

—Unknown

6. **Creators**—Anyone can consume information, but that doesn't equate to learning. The Center for Accelerated Learning notes:

    Learning is creation, not consumption. Knowledge is not something a learner absorbs, but something a learner creates. Learning happens when a learner integrates new knowledge and skill into his or her existing structure of self. Learning is literally a matter of creating new meanings, new neural networks, and new patterns of electro/chemical interactions within one's total brain/body system.[8]

    For Lisa, the biggest shift in her classroom was from teacher-centric instruction to learner-centric creation. While many students in her class might have been able to regurgitate or re-share their understanding of mitosis, Lisa wanted them to really understand the concept and retain the knowledge. Creating something helped them make a personal connection to the information—an important key for deeper learning. Those connections need to happen every day in our schools. From a teaching standpoint, Lisa focused on the creation of new ideas, which led to the creation of new content and knowledge by the students. *Creation* is crucial.

    With access to a plethora of digital resources and information, it's important to foster a culture of creation versus consumption. Instilling the idea of creation is especially important in light of the growing popularity of the "flipped classroom," in which students watch some sort of video or connect with a resource at home and do their "homework" at school. The thing is that, whether delivered in person or through a video, the lecture focuses on the consumption of information. What if the "flip" was, instead of students watching a video, they created one in which they shared the objectives they needed to grasp? Consider how much deeper learning could be if "creation" was a non-negotiable in the learning for both us and our students.

7. **Resilient**—I love the Chinese proverb that says, "The person who says it cannot be done should not interrupt the person doing it." Oh, if only an innovative educator's life were that easy!

    For those with an innovator's mindset, the reality is that their work will constantly be questioned simply because it is something new. Most people are far more comfortable with a known average than with dealing with the unknown—even if the unknown

IF YOU DON'T BELIEVE IN YOUR IDEA, WHY WOULD ANYONE ELSE?

#InnovatorsMindset

holds great possibility. Innovators will get pushback in the form of comments like, "Let's not throw out the baby with the bathwater." Objections like this are really meant to disguise people's fear of moving forward. With that in mind, innovators must be prepared to move forward, even when the risk of rejection is involved.

In Lisa's example, she ran the risk of her colleagues questioning the wisdom of going outside the lines. Or her administration might have expressed concern about the implications of students sharing their work on YouTube (even though many students already have a presence on there or other social media platforms).

Anything new and different can seem threatening. One thing I have learned is that, when thinking about moving forward, focusing on the question, "What is best for learners?" helps ensure you're making the right decisions.

Aside from concerns expressed by colleagues, you may face pushback on new ideas from your students. As stated earlier, many students are so accustomed to school that projects that veer outside the traditional lines of education terrify them. School can easily become a checklist for our students (complete homework, tests, rubrics, graduation requirements, etc.). In contrast to multiple choice tests, learning that focuses on creation and powerful connections to concepts not only takes more effort but also more time. Yet, if we do not challenge our students in their learning experiences, we aren't truly preparing them for the real world. Yes, it is important, if not crucial, to listen and respond to our students' input, but it is equally important to help them become resilient and face adversity. The school environment is the perfect place to challenge and encourage them to stretch their thinking; and it's a safe place for them to try, fail, and try again.

Resilience is a necessary trait for innovators, but it's also a skill that all humans need to develop. Life is full of ups and downs. How you recover from failure and move forward is important to how you learn and how you live. As you push the edges of the norm with your innovative ideas, hold onto your conviction and passion. If you don't believe in your idea, why would anyone else?

8. **Reflective**—Reflection, not only in innovation but also in education, is a practice to which we need to pay more attention. It is a process that is crucial to innovation, as it ensures we're asking valuable questions, such as "What worked? What didn't? What would I/we change? What questions do I have moving forward?"

Questioning our efforts, progress, and processes is crucial to innovation. By constantly revisiting our learning in any space, we find areas that can be tweaked, modified, reiterated, or even rein-vented. Looking back is crucial to moving forward. Reflection also helps us, as educators, to make our own connections, and again, deepen our learning.

In education, how often do we actually build in reflection to our learning? We have a lot of schools that do variations of "Drop Everything and Read" (DEAR), a concept that encourages stu-dents to read and consume information. But few schools focus on encouraging students or educators to "Drop Everything and *Reflect*." How might we all be impacted if we took time out of each day to the think about what we have learned and how it impacts our next steps?

HOW DOES AN INNOVATOR'S MINDSET AFFECT STUDENTS?

The hope that our students become innovators in schools that do not have educators who embody the same mindset is, at best, wishful thinking. If we do not model these characteristics and the willingness to innovate inside of the box, why would our students do anything different? They won't.

We cannot limit innovation. Trying things that push us out of our comfort zone while determining every step our students take in our classrooms will not help them think differently. It is essential that we learn when to step in and when to step aside and allow—and even cre-ate—opportunities for our students to come up with their own types of learning opportunities.

If you go on to social media platforms, like YouTube or Vine, you will see students creating things we never could have imagined in our younger years. When I see these amazing creations, I always wonder whether these students are creating and developing these innovative ideas *because of* or *in spite of schools*? Our role is to empower students to see themselves as innovators who take responsibility for their own learning and leading.

What we model is what we get.

—Jimmy Casas

As leaders, we cannot tell others they should be innovative while we continue to do the same thing. The characteristics we look for in our teachers and our students—empathizing, problem finding and solving, risk-taking, networking, observing, creating, bouncing back, and reflecting—should be embodied in our work as well. As a principal, I did not simply recreate what my former principals did. Instead, I constantly asked the question, "Would I want to be in a community where I was the principal?" Working from that empathetic mindset, allowed me to keep the teachers' perspective in mind. There were lots of things that I took from my former administrators, but, I will have to admit, there are some things I chose not to replicate because I hated them as a teacher. If I hated them, why would my staff enjoy them?

Working with Lisa reminded me that educators are not scared of change, but they don't always feel supported to take the risks in the first place. It's crucial for administrators to understand that *having support* and *feeling supported* are two different things. Administrators often encourage risks while refusing to take chances themselves. Taking risks is also different from "openly taking risks," where your team can see that you are willing to go out of your way to be an innovator as well. If an administrator takes a risk that no one can see, does anyone learn from it? Probably not. Leaders, whatever their role, will more easily affect change if they allow others to see them taking risks, failing, recovering, and risking all over again.

A NEW WAY OF THINKING

In preparation to write this chapter, I followed up with Lisa once more. She told me that her shift in thinking has changed everything for her and her students. All it took for her to rethink her teaching was a single opportunity to do something new and experience some success. And that's a key lesson: innovation is not about changing everything; sometimes you only need to change one thing. That experience can lead to new and better learning opportunities.

MOVING FORWARD

As we close out this chapter, I want to share what I call the **mantra of an innovative educator.**

I am an educator.

I am an innovator.

I am an innovative educator and I will continue to ask, "What is best for learners?" With this empathetic approach, I will create and design learning experiences.

I believe that my abilities, intelligence, and talents can be developed, leading to the creation of new and better ideas.

I recognize that there are obstacles in education, but, as an innovator, I will focus on what is possible today and where I can push to lead towards tomorrow.

I will utilize the tools that are available to me today, and I will continue to search for new and better ways to grow, develop, and share my thinking, while creating and connecting my learning.

I focus not only on where I can improve, but where I am already strong, and I look to develop those strengths in myself and in others.

I build upon what I already know, but I do not limit myself. I'm open to and willing to embrace new learning, while continuously asking questions that help me move forward.

I question thinking, challenge ideas, and do not accept, "This is the way we have always done it" as an acceptable answer for our students or myself.

I model the learning and leadership I seek in others. I take risks, try new things to develop, and explore new opportunities. I ask others to take risks in their learning, and I openly model that I'm willing to do the same.

I believe that isolation is the enemy of innovation, and I will learn from others to create better learning opportunities for others and myself.

I connect with others both locally and globally to tap into ideas from all people and spaces. I will use those ideas, along with my professional judgment, to adapt the ideas to meet the needs of the learners in my community.

I believe in my voice and experiences, as well as the voice and experiences of others, as they are important for moving education forward.

I share because the learning I create and the experiences I have help others. I share to push my own thinking and to make an impact on learners, both young and old, all over the world.

I listen and learn from different perspectives because I know we are much better together than we could ever be alone. I can learn from anyone and any situation.

I actively reflect on my learning because I know looking back is crucial to moving forward.

If we all embrace this mindset, imagine what education could become.

QUESTIONS FOR DISCUSSION

1. What risk might you take to change learning experiences?

2. How might you create an environment that fosters risk-taking?

3. How do you exhibit the innovator's mindset in the learning and work that you do currently?

NOTES

1. Lisa Jones, Twitter post, October 30, 2014, 6:09 a.m., https://twitter.com/lisat_jones/statuses/527809537164988416.

2. George Couros, "8 Characteristics of the 'Innovator's Mindset,'" *The Principal of Change: Stories of Leading and Learning*, September 16, 2014, http://georgecouros.ca/blog/archives/4783.

3. Image used with permission from Sylvia Duckworth, @sylviaduckworth, https://www.flickr.com/photos/15664662@N02/.

4. Ewan McIntosh, "TEDx London – Ewan McIntosh," YouTube video, 8:01, November 18, 2011, https://www.youtube.com/watch?v=JUnhyyw8_kY.

5. Tom Kaneshige, "How 'Liquid Networks' Can Lead to the Next Great Idea," *CIO*, April 29, 2014, http://www.cio.com/article/2376694/innovation/how--liquid-networks--can-lead-to-the-next-great-idea.html.

6. Clive Thompson, "Why Even the Worst Bloggers Are Making Us Smarter." *WIRED*, September 17, 2013, http://www.wired.com/2013/09/how-successful-networks-nurture-good-ideas-2/.

7. Chris Anderson, "How Web Video Powers Global Innovation," TED Talk, 18:53, July 2010, http://www.ted.com/talks/.chris_anderson_how_web_video_powers_global_innovation#t-187404.

8. Alcenter, "What Is Accelerated Learning?" *Alcenter.com*, accessed July 13, 2015, http://www.alcenter.com/whatisal.html.

PART II:
LAYING THE
GROUNDWORK

In Part 1, we discussed why innovation is important, what it means, and what it could look like. This vision is crucial but means little without action.

In Part II, we will turn our attention toward creating the conditions that empower a culture of learning and innovation in your school or district. We'll start by looking at how to build powerful relationships in our organizations because, without those, we have nothing. We will then discuss why leaders must be continual learners if they are to be innovators. From there we'll examine why shifting from engagement to empowerment benefits of all learners. Finally, you'll be encouraged to co-create a shared vision for learning with your community. By working together, we can create better opportunities for all learners.

CHAPTER 4
RELATIONSHIPS, RELATIONSHIPS, RELATIONSHIPS

We need to build more organizations that prioritize the care of human beings. As leaders, it is our sole responsibility to protect our people and, in turn, our people will protect each other and advance the organization together. As employees or members of the group, we need the courage to take care of each other when our leaders don't. And in doing so, we become the leaders we wish we had.

–Simon Sinek[1]

You have probably had this experience.

Frustrated with a company, you call its toll-free number to talk to someone to get a problem sorted out. You press "zero" to bypass the recorded options and talk to a real-live person. (Nobody wants to listen to a machine when they are frustrated.) You wait on hold, *finally* get through to a representative and share your issue, only to be told that, while he would love to help you, the only person who can resolve your issue is the "manager." The longer you're on hold, the more upset you feel. By the time the manager takes your call, your expectations have simultaneously lowered and increased: You expect more because of the time you have wasted, but you expect less because you have wasted so much time. If you could jump ship to another company, you would.

It's an all-too-common scenario. The people who deal with the customers don't have the power to help them. But the representatives' inability to resolve your issue isn't their fault. It's a *leadership* problem. In those companies, the "customer service representative" isn't trusted to do the right thing.

Fortunately, there are some companies whose leaders understand the importance of empowering their workers. Recently, I was at Starbucks (actually, while sitting there and writing this book) and bought one of their "protein packs." I took a bite out of an egg, which didn't sit too well with me. I immediately went up to the counter and explained the problem. The person I spoke to (who was not a manager) refunded my money and gave me an alternative item for free. That simply, my issue was resolved and my loyalty to the company was

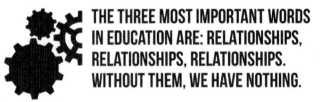

THE THREE MOST IMPORTANT WORDS IN EDUCATION ARE: RELATIONSHIPS, RELATIONSHIPS, RELATIONSHIPS. WITHOUT THEM, WE HAVE NOTHING.

reaffirmed. Starbucks' employees are given the freedom to take ownership of their work. That's one of the reasons I go there, and it's one of the reasons Starbucks consistently is ranked as one of the best places to work.[2]

But what does this have to do with innovation?

Everything.

If you are not trusted to make a common-sense decision, why would you go above and beyond to become innovative?

Stephen Covey, leadership expert and author of *The Speed of Trust*, explains how trust, or lack thereof, can have a significant impact on performance in business. His message also applies to education:

When trust is low, in a company or in a relationship, it places a hidden "tax" on every transaction: every communication, every interaction, every strategy, every decision is taxed, bringing speed down and sending costs up. My experience is that significant distrust doubles the cost of doing business and triples the time it takes to get things done.

By contrast, individuals and organizations that have earned and operated with high trust experience the opposite of a tax—a "dividend" that is like a performance multiplier, enabling them to succeed in their communications, interactions, and decisions and to move with incredible speed. A recent Watson Wyatt study showed that high-trust companies outperform low-trust companies by nearly 300 percent![3]

As leaders in education, our job is not to control those whom we serve but to unleash their talent. If innovation is going to be a priority in education, we need to create a culture where trust is the norm. This must be modeled at the highest level of the organization if we expect teachers to create the same culture in their classrooms. In some cases, that may mean we, as leaders, have to extend trust to our people before they've "earned" it. But it's far easier to trust someone when you have a relationship with that person.

As you think about your role as an educational leader and the level of trust in your school or district, consider the following questions:

- Do people often ask me for permission or guidance?
- Have I created an environment where risks are not only encouraged but expected?
- How have I highlighted the great work being done by our school to others in and out of the organization?

These questions are about innovation, but they're also the importance of relationships in creating a "culture of innovation." In fact, relationships are crucial for innovation, which is why you'll always hear me say that the three most important words in education are: relationships, relationships, relationships. Without them, we have nothing.

THE POWER TO KILL INNOVATION

Matt Gomez, an innovative kindergarten teacher from Texas, created a private Facebook page in 2010 to share the happenings of his classroom with parents (which I was later granted access to). Today, this teacher's initiative may not seem *innovative*; communicating through social media is the norm for many educators. At the time, however, it was one of the first instances where I had seen a kindergarten teacher use this medium to connect with and actually calm parents. Matt told me that, initially, some parents expressed reluctance, which is normal for anyone trying something new. But they gave him their trust. By the end of the year, Matt's parents loved seeing the work that was happening in his classroom. Below are just a few of the raving comments he received from parents on the class's Facebook page:

"Just watched this and got goosebumps. Thank you for going the extra mile to share Julie's (and your classroom's) educational experiences with our family. It has been an answered prayer to know Julie had such a wonderful teacher and great start to her education."

"Mr. Gomez, as a first-time kindergarten parent, I was very concerned about how my child would do all day in school. Your Facebook page has given me the peace of mind to know that she is having a fun day, filled with learning and growth. Also, with your lessons that are posted on here, it gives us parents a heads-up on the standard what-did-you-do-today answer of 'nothing.' We now know what they did and can easily engage them in further expansion of that lesson, class project, etc. I really do thank you for all you have done for our children and us parents. I will miss our Facebook next school year..."

"Any chance the 1st grade teachers will have a Facebook page?"

Powerful, huh? Notice that parents' perceptions shifted from concern to praise. Matt's risk paid off. He used the tool to connect with parents in an extremely meaningful way, and the reassurance these kindergarten parents (some who have never before had a child in school) experienced was powerful. Beyond that, the parents and teachers worked together (in a space that they are all in, anyway), created relationships, and learned about classroom initiatives, all while they modeled for students a positive digital identity.

Unfortunately, Matt was asked by his administration to no longer partake in this activity. Matt explained to his students' parents:

> *My class Facebook page is shutting down this week. I was told that the district does not support it and thus must close it down. I knew this might happen; it was a risk I took in trying something so unknown without permission. I had prepared myself for this day. The page was very successful, and I feel I met my goal of showing that there is more we can do to engage parents. Actually, the success of the page is what led to its demise. The great teachers I work with also wanted to use the tool, and parents began to ask why I was the only one using it. This made my principal need to address the situation, and the final solution is closing it down.*

EQUITY AT THE HIGHEST LEVEL

One of the concerns Matt's administrators shared was that, because what he was doing was so successful, they feared it would put more pressure on others in the building. Years ago, another educator shared a similar story, explaining that she wanted to try something new called "blogging." The teacher asked her principal if she could try it out and, at the time, was told "no." The reason? The principal was concerned that if the venture succeeded, everyone on staff would be expected to do it.

What?

At least the leaders in these two cases were brave enough to say what many others think but never verbalize. The fear that drives leaders is not always about failure. Sometimes, the real fear is of success. If something works, other educators in the building would be expected to do it, thus creating more work for everyone.

Another concern often voiced in response to innovative initiatives is that the new program or approach might create superior learning opportunities—opportunities that aren't offered in another learning environment. If what's best for learners is our primary concern, equity of opportunities will be created at the highest of levels, not the lowest.

THE POWER OF "NO" VERSUS A CULTURE OF "YES"

The problem is that when you say "no" to innovation—for any reason—people feel reluctant to attempt trying new things in the future. Their thinking is, "If I am not allowed to do something that could impact learning in my classroom or other classrooms, what purpose do I have in serving the needs of the school as a whole?" In other words, they think, *"My ideas don't matter."* And the innovation-squelching effect of *no* spreads like wildfire. When one staff member hears that someone was thwarted in their attempt to try something new, others learn to either not bother or become subversive. Some brave souls forge ahead, working from the belief that it's better to ask for forgiveness rather than permission. But if we've established a culture in which educators feel their only option is to ask forgiveness for trying new things, this is not an educator issue, it's a *leadership* issue. To quote Steve Jobs, "It doesn't make sense to hire smart people and then tell them what to do; we hire smart people so they can tell us what to do." If leaders spend the majority of time trying to manage and protect people from their own mistakes, not only are they wasting time, but they are losing the confidence of those they serve.

Squashing the ambitions of those who want to go above and beyond to try something new will ensure schools have only "pockets of innovation," at best, and, at worst, no innovation. Sooner or later, the innovators will get tired of asking for forgiveness. They'll move on to places where they're trusted to use their creativity and passion—or, perhaps worse, they'll settle into the status quo. In either case, learners will be deprived of their ingenuity.

Rather than limiting educators' initiative, and thereby students' learning opportunities, let's create environments of *competitive collaboration*, where educators at all levels push and help one another to become better. For this to happen, ideas need to be shared openly

> ## IF WHAT'S BEST FOR LEARNERS IS OUR PRIMARY CONCERN, EQUITY OF OPPORTUNITIES WILL BE CREATED AT THE HIGHEST OF LEVELS, NOT THE LOWEST.

and consistently (something that will be discussed more in Chapter 11, "Embracing an Open Culture"), not hidden for fear of being shut down. Likewise, we must build and strengthen relationships with (and between) our educators so that every individual sees him or herself as an integral part of a larger whole.

Instead of fear driving us to a place where "no" is our default, we need to strive to create a "culture of yes." When trust is the norm and people know they are supported, taking chances seems less "risky"—for learners, educators, and leaders. That doesn't mean we should blindly say yes to everything, but it's important to remember that saying *yes* allows us to find ways to make innovation happen.

CLASSROOM TEACHER VERSUS THE SCHOOL TEACHER

When I first started teaching, I was told by some teachers that I shouldn't expect my colleagues to be eager to share their work. It seems there are some educators who feel reluctant to hand over work that has taken them hours, days, or even years to develop for their students.

Luckily, my first teaching partner willingly gave me everything she had already developed (thanks, Marlene!). Her generosity was a tremendous help and set me on a path that would have looked much different if she had chosen not to share.

The differing viewpoints here are of the *classroom teacher* and *school teacher*. Classroom teachers are those who do great things within their classroom and will do great things with their students. School teachers do all of the above. The difference is school teachers consider every student in the school as their own, no matter if that child is in their grade or subject at the time. School teachers see things like supervision as an opportunity, not a chore, because it is a time to connect with other students and get to know them on a different level.

School teachers are also willing to share their ideas. If I am doing something innovative in my classroom, sharing it with my colleagues benefits their students as well. Even if other teachers don't use my suggestions or ideas the same way I do, the simple act of sharing sparks creativity as we tweak, alter, and remix what we and others do.

This collaborative spirit is a trait that both teachers *and* administrators should embody. One of my mentors and a long-time principal in Parkland School Division, Dr. David Pysyk, taught me a lesson early in my career as a school administrator. He told me he went out of his way every morning to stand in the front foyer of the school and greet kids and staff as they came in the building. I can't count the number of times Dr. Pysyk's staff and students commented on his routine. This little gesture by the principal made a statement to everyone that the school was about the students. He viewed greeting them each morning not as job but as an opportunity. And his example immediately set the tone for the school. As a result, staff members stood outside their classrooms, connected with students in hallways, and created relationships with the kids and one another. If you are a superintendent, principal, coach, teacher, or serve any other role inside of a school, let people know you are about the kids; you are setting the tone for your school.

CHANGE CAN HAPPEN ONE PERSON AT A TIME

Staff professional development can provide opportunities for creating a shared understanding of the group as a whole, but we also have to remember that the *whole* is made up of *individuals*. I have been in schools where everyone received the same book to read and learn from together. This standardized approach assumes the educator hasn't already read the book, the content is relevant to everyone, and everyone has the same needs to move forward. That's a lot of assumptions.

What if we took a different, more personalized approach? Legendary professional basketball coach Phil Jackson (who has more championships than any other professional basketball coach) won by tapping into the strengths of the individuals. Each played specific roles that were part of, and important to, the team as a whole. One of the things he did to meet his players' personal developmental needs was to provide each member of his team with a different book based on what he thought would help that player's journey.

Imagine knowing individuals in such a way that you could actually select specific materials to accommodate that staff member's needs and interests. Not only would you be able to help each person improve in his or her work and career goals, but you would also show that you

DO YOU SEE THE PERSONAL MOMENTS YOU HAVE WITH YOUR STAFF AS INVESTMENTS OR EXPENDITURES?

#InnovatorsMindset

know and care about each person you serve on a deeper level. It would also model an attitude that could easily trickle down to the classroom level and each individual student.

Culture is developed by the expectations, interactions, and, ultimately, the relationships of the entire learning community. But relationships are built one-on-one. Do you see the personal moments you have with your staff as investments or expenditures? Ten minutes spent listening to someone who is dealing with a personal issue will do wonders from a leadership perspective to instill loyalty in that person, as well as a willingness to go above and beyond what is expected. Those moments are investments in the relationships that foster a culture of innovation.

In a *New Yorker* article titled "Slow Ideas," surgeon and public health researcher Atul Gawande explained why one-on-one interactions increase people's willingness to try something new.

> But technology and incentive programs are not enough. "Diffusion is essentially a social process through which people talking to people spread an innovation," wrote Everett Rogers, the great scholar of how new ideas are communicated and spread. Mass media can introduce a new idea to people. But, Rogers showed, people follow the lead of other people they know and trust when they decide whether to take it up. Every change requires effort, and the decision to make that effort is a social process.
>
> This is something that salespeople understand well. I once asked a pharmaceutical rep how he persuaded doctors—who are notoriously stubborn—to adopt a new medicine. Evidence is not remotely enough, he said, however strong a case you may have. You must also apply "the rule of seven touches." Personally "touch" the doctors seven times, and they will come to know you; if they know you, they might trust you; and, if they trust you, they will change. That's why he stocked doctors' closets with free drug samples in person. Then he could poke his head around the corner and ask, "So how did your daughter Debbie's soccer game go?" Eventually, this can become "Have you seen this study on our new drug? How about giving it a try?" As the rep had recognized, human

interaction is the key force in overcoming resistance and speeding change.[4]

This article helped shift my thinking regarding how we do professional learning. As division principal within Parkland School Division in Alberta, Canada, serving twenty-two schools and more than 10,000 students, it is easy to try to think about how to spread and develop great ideas quickly. One of the challenges with the large group workshop model is that, no matter how hard we try to differentiate, not everyone will get out of the day what you (or they) might hope. There are times when large group sessions are necessary to develop a shared vision. But to move people from their point A to their point B, I believe it is necessary, as Gawande mentions, to create regular opportunities for human interaction that help build relationships and spur innovation.

For example, as a central office administrator, I often visited schools and held the equivalent of college professor office hours. Throughout the day, I booked several forty- to sixty-minute sessions with one to three staff members at a time. These smaller groups helped create an intimacy that is often lacking in many of our larger, one-size-fits-all learning opportunities and allowed me to get to know participants in a much better way. It also created opportunities for each staff member to get to know one another. The sessions were open-ended and we tailored the discussions based on the simple question, "What would you like to learn?" We focused on what the learner wanted, not on what I wanted to deliver. In some of the sessions, I shared tools to make communication easier. In other sessions, we talked about the shifting philosophies on how to teach. There was no set agenda for the sessions, since each was focused on the needs of the teacher-learner. But as the individuals left my temporary office, they felt heard, they felt as if I cared about them and their personal success, and they had learned something that was important to them. These "touches" helped build relationships across the division and amongst teachers, which are foundational to our culture of learning and innovation.

Now, you may be thinking that this individual approach to creating a culture of innovation would take forever—especially in larger districts. It may even seem impossible to meet with everyone, one by one. And to be honest, if that's what you're thinking, you are right. I thought the same thing, and I knew it was impossible to meet with every educator in the school division. What I noticed, though, was how these one-on-one sessions accelerated innovation. Instead of people relying on me to create the learning experiences, each staff member I'd met with saw the value in the ideas we discussed and found a new confidence to share those ideas with other colleagues. Some even led their own sessions on what they had learned. One principal told me that a staff member, who had never shared anything during their professional learning, pleaded to have time to share what she had learned and how it was impacting her students.

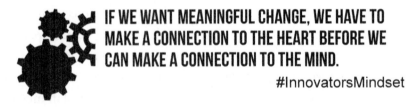

IF WE WANT MEANINGFUL CHANGE, WE HAVE TO MAKE A CONNECTION TO THE HEART BEFORE WE CAN MAKE A CONNECTION TO THE MIND.

#InnovatorsMindset

Our job, sometimes, is simply to be the spark, help build confidence, and then get out of the way. If innovation in any school or school division is solely dependent upon one person, it will continue to happen in pockets. In contrast, when we focus on empowering learners to become leaders, they help spread ideas. Sometimes, empowering just one person is all it takes to push an entire group.

MOVING FORWARD

If we want meaningful change, we have to make a connection to the heart before we can make a connection to the mind. Spending time developing relationships and building trust is crucial to moving forward as a whole. Without *culture*, there is no culture of innovation. It all starts by creating an environment where people feel cared for, supported, and nurtured—the very things we know that impact learning for students in the classroom.

In a world where digital interaction is the norm, we crave human interaction more than ever. That's why the three things you need to ensure innovation flourishes in your organization are relationships, relationships, and relationships. Fifty years ago, relationships were the most important thing in our schools, and fifty years from now, it will be no different.

QUESTIONS FOR DISCUSSION

1. How do you build relationships with individuals in your district, school, and classroom?

2. How do you empower others to take risks? Examples?

3. How do you create opportunities for your school community to have learning driven by their personal interests?

NOTES

1. Simon Sinek, *Leaders Eat Last: Why Some Teams Pull Together and Others Don't* (New York: Portfolio/Penguin, 2014), 18.

2. Starbucks Newsroom, "Starbucks Named One of the Top 10 Places to Work in Canada," *News.Starbucks.com*, April 10, 2015, https://news.starbucks.com/news/starbucks-named-one-of-the-top-10-places-to-work-in-canada.

3. Stephen M. R. Covey, "How the Best Leaders Build Trust," *Leadershipnow.com*, accessed July 15, 2015, http://www.leadershipnow.com/CoveyOnTrust.html.

4. Atul Gawande, "Spreading Slow Ideas," *The New Yorker*, July 29, 2013, http://www.newyorker.com/magazine/2013/07/29/slow-ideas.

CHAPTER 5
LEARN, LEAD, INNOVATE

Why are we okay that management hasn't seen innovation in one hundred or fifty years, but we demand innovation in every other aspect of our lives?

—Jamie Notter

hen I was a kid, my parents could only afford to phone their family in Greece once a month. Calling long-distance, especially overseas, was expensive. I remember watching futuristic shows like *The Jetsons* and imagining the day when video phones would allow me to actually see my relatives' faces. Today with video technologies like FaceTime, Skype, and Google Hangouts, it's easy and inexpensive to stay in touch with friends and family around the world. And yet, now that this amazing capability is in our hands, many adults do not make a big deal of it—some even complain about people being constantly connected, particularly as it relates to education. It's true that one could argue that innovations in technology have created a world in which the ability to be constantly connected distracts kids and interrupts the way we teach. Then there's another viewpoint, one that realizes our students' ability to connect with people, anytime and anywhere, creates many new opportunities for learning.

The way you view change—in education, technology, and *life*—shapes the way you lead. Yet, too often, change is something we talk about and expect of others, not necessarily ourselves. If we're going to be effective leaders, we must model the behavior and attitudes we seek in our learners—be they students or educators. After all, it is much more powerful and persuasive to say, "Let's do this together!" than to command people to do something we're not willing or able to do ourselves.

DISRUPT YOUR ROUTINE

One of the best ways for leaders to take notice of, and even discover, new and better opportunities is to experience life from the end users' viewpoint. Frank Barrett, an organizational behavior expert, explains that disrupting routines and looking at a situation from another's perspective can lead to new solutions. In a *Harvard Business Review* video titled "To Innovate, Disrupt Your Routine,"[1] Barrett shares the story of an airline that was dealing with many complaints about their customer service. The airline's leaders held a retreat with the intention of focusing on how to create a better experience for their customers. While everyone else was in meetings on the first day of the retreat, the airline's vice president of marketing had the beds in each leader's hotel room replaced with airline seats. The next day, after having spent the night in airline seats, the company's leaders came up with some "radical innovations" on how to improve their customers' comfort. Had the VP of marketing not disrupted their sleeping routines and allowed them to experience their customers' discomfort, the retreat may have well ended without any noteworthy or innovative changes.

The customers are the end users in business. For us as educational leaders, our learners are the end users. And sometimes experiencing their discomfort in our schools and classrooms can be eye-opening. Case in point: Grant Wiggins, visionary education reformer and one of the developers of the *Understanding by Design Framework*, shared a powerful guest post on his blog, written by an educator who shadowed two students, each for a day, in her new school.[2] Here was the initial plan as described by the writer:

> As part of getting my feet wet, my principal suggested I "be" a student for two days: I was to shadow and complete all the work of a tenth-grade student on one day and to do the same for a twelfth-grade student on another day. My task was to do everything the student was supposed to do: if there was a lecture or notes on the board, I copied them as fast I could into my notebook. If there was a chemistry lab, I did it with my host student. If there was a test, I took it (I passed the Spanish one, but I am certain I failed the business one).

The post was telling as she shared how she struggled through the process of "being a student." Upon completing the two days, she notes the following key takeaways:

1. Students sit all day, and sitting is exhausting.
2. High school students are sitting passively and listening during approximately ninety percent of their classes.
3. You feel a little bit like a nuisance all day long.

Now, the point of sharing this is not to challenge her ideas—this is from the perspective of her school at the time—but to think about what we *really* know about our students' experiences while in school. How often do we make assumptions about what is happening in our schools? And could it be, as this educator found, that our assumptions may be inaccurate or incomplete? We've got to keep asking ourselves the question I posed earlier: *Would I want to be a learner in my own classroom?* If you look at education from this viewpoint, you might find that some of the expectations put on our students are not something you or I could handle for an hour, let alone a full day.

One quote from the blog post about a student's perspective of her class really shook me. "I asked my tenth-grade host, Cindy, if she felt like she made important contributions to class or if, when she was absent, the class missed out on the benefit of her knowledge or contributions, and she laughed and said, 'No.'"

Can you imagine going to a place every day where you felt your voice didn't matter? I was struck by this takeaway in particular. It made me realize that so many students share this experience of having almost no autonomy and very little opportunity to directly choose their learning experiences.

The reality of schools is that learning environments are not created solely by the teacher but by the entire staff. If this is what students experience when they come to our schools, what might we do as leaders to help support learning and innovation to create something new and better?

BE PRESENT, LEAD PEOPLE, MANAGE THINGS

One of my own intentions as a central office administrator was to support our educators by being in the schools as much as possible. I felt that, to lead a culture of innovation, it was crucial for me to be connected to the work teachers were doing. My thought was: if my decisions had an impact on classrooms, then I wanted to immerse myself in the learning environment to inform those decisions.

I often took my laptop and would sit in a classroom for anywhere from three to six hours. While I worked on administrative tasks and answered emails, the teachers and students went about their day and eventually forgot I was there. Being physically present in the classroom helped me develop a better understanding of the experiences of the teachers and students. I wasn't there to evaluate the teachers. In fact, it was more about evaluating the environment that the school district had created. One thing I noticed during that time is how much "other stuff" teachers had to do to make things work. Whether it was going through an arduous computer logon process with students, or dealing with constant issues with wifi, they looked less like teachers and more like magicians. And yet, time and again, I saw frustrated educators go above and beyond to create powerful learning opportunities for our students.

If we want "innovation" to flourish in our schools, we have to be willing to immerse ourselves in the environments where it is going to happen. If you're thinking you don't have the time, remember that your technology is *mobile*. You can do what I did; take your computer or tablet and work while you're in the classrooms. I might be able to answer my email a lot faster in my quiet office, but there are so many reasons why I would rather do it in the classroom. Being able to discuss the realities of teaching and learning is chief among those reasons.

Another thing we must be willing to do is remove barriers that challenge those we serve. For example, I mentioned the time-consuming logon process for students. From an IT department perspective, getting Internet access is often fast, and the logon process is quick. But when you consider that each class has twenty to thirty students in a classroom (if you are lucky), what seems quick and easy for one person in the IT office may take several minutes for the entire class to accomplish. This is especially pertinent in a classroom where time is often limited and every minute counts. This is one of many examples of how being present in the classroom allowed me to understand the realities of our teachers' experiences. Had I not seen for myself how that time adds up, I might not have had the same appreciation of this particular challenge.

The educators we serve need the tools and resources to work if we truly want to create a culture of innovation. They also need to feel our support in creating an environment that we would truly want to be in as learners ourselves. As leaders, we must have a vision for our schools, educators, and learners. At the same time, we must manage the things that will support our educators as we work together to make that vision a reality. As Stephen R. Covey said, "You manage things, but you lead people. That is how we will empower them."[3]

MASTER LEARNER, INNOVATIVE LEADER

Being present in the classroom reminded me that it is my job to learn first if I want to lead well. As leaders and innovators, it can be easy to want to rush into change before we've taken the time to really explore what that change could and should look like. Here's an example of what I'm talking about: Several years ago, I started hearing about "digital portfolios" from educators who wanted to try them with their students. The problem was most of these educators had never actually gone through the process of creating a digital portfolio themselves. As a teacher, they liked the concept. The problem was that they didn't stop to consider how digital portfolios would work from the learner's viewpoint. As I have watched this process unfold in many schools, what I saw were paper portfolios done digitally. In many cases, they look like a "digital dump" where kids simply share links to their work.

I wanted to figure out what a digital portfolio could be and how it could be used for teaching and, more importantly, for learning. Rather than asking my staff and students to do something I'd yet to experience myself, I decided I needed to create my own digital portfolio and explore the process's merits, challenges, and potential.

I started my own blog to begin, which is a "portfolio" of my learning. I learned about the power of open reflection and how it can deepen learning. When I know everyone can see my work and reflections, it makes me think more deeply about what I'm learning. My blog also led me to see the power of collaboration, not only within the school but also globally. Anyone, from anywhere in the world, could challenge my ideas, which, in turn, challenged my thinking. I discovered that a portfolio should be a showcase of one's learning as well as a vehicle for it. Through the process of learning openly, I also started to understand the impact of my digital footprint. I also learned what it meant to actually *have* a digital footprint and could discuss the benefits and ramifications with my students from a real-life perspective, rather than simply share other people's research. What better way to build credibility with our students than to actually *do* what we're teaching them to do?

What started as one portfolio (my own) led to an entire school creating engaging, learner-focused digital portfolios. Now Parkland School Division is in the process of implementing digital portfolios with all schools. By no means do I take the credit for the rollout, as we have a very forward-thinking and hardworking staff within our schools that supported this work, but being able to learn and then teach from experience helped get the ball rolling. The result of personal learning led to providing more than 10,000 students with the ability and opportunity to have a digital portfolio that they create, develop, and maintain in some form from kindergarten to grade twelve. This is still a work in progress, and the learning can be very messy. (We need to embrace this messiness!) Our leaders understood that the sheer size of information that the students are creating and collecting would be impossible to do with paper, yet the ability to create portfolios digitally has allowed students the opportunity to curate and share their growth over time. (If you want to learn more about blogs and digital portfolios, you can check them out on my portfolio at bit.ly/blogasportfolio.)

Great leaders make a vision come to reality by being able to break the vision down into smaller steps. Each small step that is accomplished helps develop confidence and competence along the way. My own example of learning helped me connect with my own staff and ensure they saw that I had credibility as a learner myself. (I never want to have the label of "not understanding what it's like to be a teacher.") Because I'd learned and experienced the process myself, I was able to encourage my staff to push the boundaries of what we were currently doing.

Being present, learning first, and leading with the learner in mind will help you grow as an innovative leader. As we close out this chapter, I want to share a few other essential traits for innovative leaders.

THE CHARACTERISTICS OF THE INNOVATIVE LEADER

1. **Visionary**—Visionary leaders can take the powerful vision they have for their schools and break it down into what it looks like in the classroom. Creating a culture of innovation requires a series of small steps taken toward a greater vision; it doesn't develop in a single, gigantic leap. Innovative leaders help people continuously grow with small steps that build both *confidence and competence,* so they are more willing and able to become more innovative themselves.

2. **Empathetic**—New ideas start with understanding the needs of those you serve. When I first became a principal, I did not try to mirror the ideas and practices of the principals who had come before me. Instead, I thought, "If I were a teacher in this school, what would I expect of my principal?" Thinking about the learning environment from that perspective also helped me empathize with being a student in the school and a parent in the community. For example, as a teacher, I felt frustrated when I attended meetings that seemed to go nowhere and went too long. So to respect the time of others, I made sure meetings were shorter and that we spent more time learning than we did on things that could have been simply emailed. Is having a shorter meeting innovative? No. But trying to put yourself in the place of those you serve is where innovation begins.

3. **Models Learning**—I have great respect for Chris Kennedy, a superintendent in West Vancouver. He believes (and models) that leaders need to be "elbows deep in learning with their schools."

I agree! It is easy to fall into the trap of doing things that have always been done or simply going with what you know. But that kind of thinking limits everyone. If we want to do better things for students, we have to become the guinea pigs and immerse ourselves in new learning opportunities to understand how to create the necessary changes. We rarely create something different until we experience something different.

4. **Open Risk-Taker**—The term "risk-taker" has become quite cliché in education. As leaders, it's easy to promote or call for risk-taking, but it's rare to see risk-taking actually modeled. People are less likely to take risks and try new things if they don't *see* those above them in the hierarchical structure doing the same thing. If leaders want people to try new things, they have to openly show that they are willing to do the same.

WE RARELY CREATE SOMETHING DIFFERENT UNTIL WE EXPERIENCE SOMETHING DIFFERENT.

#InnovatorsMindset

5. **Networked**—Networks are imperative to growth and innovation. It is easy to think you are doing something amazing when you are not looking beyond the walls of your school. Great leaders have always created networks. It's easier than ever to connect today. Face-to-face interaction is great, but, with technology, we are no longer limited by our location or travel budget. Anyone willing to reach out is now able to connect with educators across the world. It is simply a choice. This freedom to connect with people outside our schools allows us to expand our thinking, remix others' ideas, and put new and better ideas into practice to create amazing learning experiences for our students.

6. **Observant**—Great ideas often spark other great ideas. The notion of "Genius Hour," which is an idea that has spread throughout schools all over the world, came about because educators noticed what was going on *outside* of schools and modified those ideas to meet their students' needs. The power of the Internet is that we have access to so much information from schools and other organizations. Although an idea observed in the business world might not necessarily work "as is" for a school, if we learn to connect ideas and reshape them, it could become something pretty amazing.

7. **Team Builder**—The least innovative organizations often seem to surround themselves with like-minded people. Innovation often comes from conflict and disagreement, not in an adversarial way but in a way that promotes divergent thinking. The focus is not to go with the idea of one person over another but to actually create a better idea—perhaps one that merges multiple, shared ideas. If you want to be an innovative leader, surrounding yourself with people who mirror your personality is *not* the way to get there.

8. **Always Focused on Relationships**—Innovation has become such a huge focus in schools that we often forget it is ultimately a human endeavor. Smartphones aren't innovative; the *thinking* behind creating a smartphone is where innovation happens. It is easy to lock yourself in an office, connect with people on Twitter, and appear from your room with some great idea or new thing. If you want to be an innovative *leader*, your role isn't simply to come up with new and better ideas but to involve your staff in that mission. If you have lost focus on and connection with the people in your building, even if you offer new ideas, they might not be embraced by those you lead. When people know they are valued and safe in trying new things, they are more likely to strive for something new and better.

MOVING FORWARD

An innovative leader should try to create new ideas, but it is more important that they create a culture of innovation. We often talk about empowering people and then getting out of their way, but what is often missed in the process is removing some of those barriers that they will encounter along the way. This is why it is so important to spend time in the classrooms, see what teaching and learning looks like, and then help to create a better tomorrow for our students and educators. Again though, at the heart of innovation are *people*, not stuff. If we always keep that truth at the forefront of our work, we are more likely to create an innovative culture.

QUESTIONS FOR DISCUSSION

1. What are some ways that you get in the "middle" of learning to understand the needs of those you serve?

2. What is a new learning initiative that you would like to see in your school, and how do you model this learning yourself?

3. Which characteristics of the innovative leader do you consider personal strengths? In which areas do you need to grow?

NOTES

1. Frank Barrett, "To Innovate, Disrupt Your Routine," *Harvard Business Review video*, 3:09, September 18, 2012, https://hbr.org/2012/09/to-innovate-disrupt-your-routi.html.

2. Grant Wiggins, "A Veteran Teacher Turned Coach Shadows 2 Students for 2 Days—A Sobering Lesson Learned," *Granted, and...-Thoughts on Education by Grant Wiggins* (blog), October 14, 2014, https://grantwiggins.wordpress.com/2014/10/10/a-veteran-teacher-turned-coach-shadows-2-students-for-2-days-a-sobering-lesson-learned/.

3. Stephen M. R. Covey, "Knowledge Workers: 10,000 Times the Productivity," *Stephencovey.com* (blog), April 7, 2008, http://www.stephencovey.com/blog/?p=15.

CHAPTER 6
ENGAGE VERSUS EMPOWER

As we look ahead into the next century, leaders will be those who empower others.

–Bill Gates

I had just walked off the plane in Roanoke, Virginia, and was headed to a hotel to speak at a conference. Instead of getting a car, I decided to take an Uber to the hotel since it was a quick trip. My driver showed up, courteously grabbed my bags, placed them in his trunk, and then opened my door for me. As we set out, I asked him if he knew where the hotel was, but he didn't respond. I asked him again. No response. I then tapped him on the shoulder, and he looked at me, surprised, and mouthed the words, "I'm deaf."

As we drove, I thought about how technology had provided a great opportunity for this man to create a career for himself. Driving a vehicle, he didn't need to know the directions to the hotel because they were automatically updated on his mobile device. He knew what I looked like from my Uber profile. Upon arriving at the hotel, I mouthed, "Thank you." He thanked me back, and we went our separate ways.

Later that night, I saw a post on the image-sharing site Imgur about another person who, when he discovered his Uber driver was deaf, did a quick Google search to learn how to sign "thank you." The driver was overwhelmed by the man's simple kindness of communicating with him in sign language. After reading the story, I felt annoyed that I had missed an opportunity to show my appreciation for someone who had provided such excellent service to me. The day after my talk, I arranged an Uber ride back to the airport and was lucky enough to get the same driver. As with the other day, the driver provided the exact same high-quality service. Remembering the post I'd seen, I spent my time in the back of the car learning how to sign "thank you." I did a Google search and then watched a video on YouTube to ensure I had the correct motion. At the airport, the driver took my bags out of the trunk and placed them on the curb. This time, instead of simply mouthing the words, I signed "thank you" to him, hoping I was doing it right. The expression of gratitude on his face shook me. It was simple and only took a few minutes to learn something that showed I valued my fellow human being.

Why did I do this? Honestly? Because I could.

The power we have at our fingertips to learn and create is awe-inspiring. There are many parts of this story that I could not have told in 2000—YouTube, Uber, accessing Google from a smartphone—but, today, these technologies are abundant and ubiquitous.

DO KIDS CREATE BECAUSE OF SCHOOL—OR IN SPITE OF IT?

This story reminded me of an encounter with a student at one of the schools in Parkland School Division in 2015. As I walked by the eighth grader, I noticed he was using an advanced engineering program on the computer to design a new car. It was "Innovation Week," a time when students have the opportunity to build and design projects based on areas of interest—and he was passionate about designing cars. I knew that no teacher in the building had taught this student how to

 YOUTUBE HAS BECOME THE BIGGEST LIBRARY OF INFORMATION IN THE WORLD.

#InnovatorsMindset

use this complex program or given him the idea to create the car in the first place. It was all his idea and doing. As I sat beside him and marveled at what he was creating, I asked him how he learned how to use the program. He looked at me as if I was crazy and responded with one word: YouTube.

Before I'd even asked, I knew there was a great chance he'd picked up the skill by watching YouTube—at school. He'd been given both the access and the time to explore the site and learn what he needed. YouTube has become the biggest library of information in the world. So why on earth do some schools block this learning resource from students (and in some places, even educators)?

One word.

Control.

A CULTURE OF COMPLIANCE

In Seth Godin's 2012 TEDx Talk entitled "Stop Stealing Dreams," he opened with the normal school morning greeting, "Good morning boys and girls!" He then said his expectation was for the audience to respond, as students have for more than one hundred years, "Good morning Mr. Godin." He explained that this statement and response, that are so normal in our classrooms, are all about creating a culture of compliance.[1] He's right. If I, as the teacher, say something to you, I expect for you to respond in a certain way. If I don't like the emphasis of your response, I will say it again, until I hear from you, the class, what I expect. The goal of the repetition is that students hear so they can repeat, not learn. But is repetition really what school is for?

I hope not.

Educators often talk about the idea of engagement and how important that is in our world today. Many have made efforts to show kids relevant and real-life examples of learning in hopes of them being more engaged in what they do. From my very early days as a teacher, I focused on engaging kids. I learned how to tell stories that were interesting and compelling. I did my best to be like Robin Williams in *Dead Poet's Society*—the teacher who captivated his students. Unfortunately, when the year ended and my "show" was over, my students' expectations for teachers were amplified. What my teaching style created was students who believed, "If you don't engage me, then you are not a good teacher." And early in my career, I'm afraid that my students and I believed that engagement was enough.

Engagement is a good thing, but I've since learned that we must also empower students and equip them with the skills to learn. It is imperative that we teach learners how to be self-directed and guide their own learning, rather than rely on others to simply engage them.

Bill Ferriter separates the idea of *engagement* and *empowerment* nicely. He states, "Engaging students means getting kids excited about our content, interests, and curricula." Empowering students "means giving kids the knowledge and skills to pursue *their* passions, interests, and future."[2]

This does not mean that empowerment happens instead of engagement. In fact, people do not feel truly empowered unless they are engaged with their learning. But if engagement is the ceiling—the highest bar—we may be missing the point. Think about it: Would you rather hear about changing the world, or do you want the opportunity

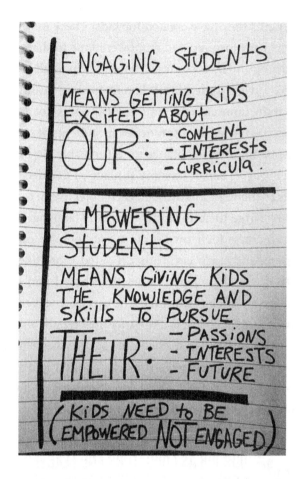

to do so? A story about a world-changer might engage us, but becoming world-changers will *change us.* So, the question for you as a professional educator is: If you had to choose between *compliant, engaged,* or *empowered,* which word would you want to define your students?

A CULTURE OF EMPOWERMENT

I'm happy to say there are many schools today in which empowerment is a focus. In fact, many of the educators with whom I have connected both locally and globally have excited and engaged *me* in the learning paths they have created for kids. These innovative teachers and leaders have inspired and empowered me to share examples of powerful learning and opportunities that can help us all move forward.

Years ago, I tried something different for our health course and was amazed at the unintentional results. Health was not a subject I was particularly excited to teach my grade seven students. It seemed almost like an "add-on," to fill in the blanks for a timetable. So instead of trying to create *engaging content* for my students, I decided to turn over the objectives to them. I went through each objective in the health curriculum and re-wrote them in student-friendly language. I then asked the students to create their own groups, pick out the objectives that interested them, and teach each other. I acted more like a professor working with doctoral students, rather than how I had envisioned a typical grade seven teacher working. The groups checked in with me daily for advice and feedback, but the way they taught and shared was so much more powerful than if I had put together some flashy lessons myself. Deep learning occurred—they understood and remembered what they taught each other. I had given my students control over their learning, and the change in atmosphere was palpable.

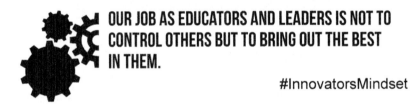

OUR JOB AS EDUCATORS AND LEADERS IS NOT TO CONTROL OTHERS BUT TO BRING OUT THE BEST IN THEM.

#InnovatorsMindset

It should be noted here that the curriculum standards were still met—I just approached them from a different perspective and allowed my students to take ownership of their learning. Up to that point, the way I had always taught (and the way I had been taught) was to learn the curriculum, create engaging lessons, and have the students show their understanding. In this model, compliance or engagement were the only two options. Empowering the students to teach the lessons created new and better opportunities for learning. As author and publisher Harriet Rubin explains, "Freedom is actually a bigger game than power. Power is about what you can control. Freedom is about what you can unleash." By empowering them, I'd unleashed my students' potential and allowed them to explore and make meaningful connections to the content to deepen their learning.

Our job as educators and leaders is not to control others but to bring out the best in them. Engagement is not enough. We need to create the same opportunities for our students as those we would want for ourselves.

IDENTITY DAY

A few years back, my assistant principal at the time, Cheryl Johnson, suggested having an "Identity Day" at our school. It was a simple idea with a major impact. On the day of the event, every person in the school—students, educators, custodians, administrative assistants, etc.—had an opportunity to share something they were passionate about with the entire school. In the first year of the event, I shared about my love of the Lakers, in the second year I talked about my dogs.

This event helped build relationships, which, I've noted, is foundational to creating an environment where people are willing to take risks, work together, and innovate. Allowing students to share their interests created an environment where they felt that their voices mattered and that what they cared about mattered as well. Students talked about their love of creating things with Legos; others shared that they wanted to be musicians and played songs they had developed. Some talked about how they wanted to be inventors and showed their latest creations.

The event gave everyone a voice and created bonds in our community that might not have been there before. For example, one of my grade two students was a national champion BMX biker, but, until that day, the majority of our school community didn't know about her talent. It was a beautiful thing to see how a grade one teacher with an interest in the same sport connected with this student. Long after the event, they talked about their favorite "extreme" sports.

One student's presentation from the first year really sticks out in my memory. A grade six student named Marley taught us about Tourette syndrome, something that she dealt with daily. No one, not even her teacher, knew she planned on presenting and teaching others about Tourette syndrome. During her presentation, she explained, "This is part of who I am, and I wanted to share it." Simple, yet powerful.

I was and am forever grateful to Cheryl Johnson for leading an opportunity that was so powerful for our community. She took a risk doing something new because she believed it would connect and empower our staff and students alike. She was right.

EMPOWERMENT IS MORE THAN A SINGLE EVENT

Today, there are so many excellent books and resources about teaching practices, such as "Genius Hour," "Makerspaces," and "Innovation Day/Week." Many educators have now heard of and embraced these ideas, and that's wonderful! Creating opportunities for students to explore their passions and interests empowers them in their learning.

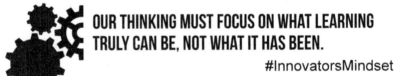

OUR THINKING MUST FOCUS ON WHAT LEARNING TRULY CAN BE, NOT WHAT IT HAS BEEN.

#InnovatorsMindset

These events help educational communities understand the power of passion-based learning—something that is as beneficial for students as it is for staff. Hosting an Innovation Day or establishing a Genius Hour is a good start, but we can't stop there. Innovation cannot be relegated to a one-off event.

Educational thought leader and co-author of the fantastic book *Invent to Learn*, Gary Stager constantly pushes the boundaries of what learning should look like—all of the time—for students. When asked about building "Makerspaces," he offered this powerful response:

> When school leaders tell me, "Our school is building a $25 million Makerspace," I am concerned that Makerspaces may exacerbate educational inequity. While there are expensive pieces of hardware that may need to be secured, I want the bulk of making to permeate every corner of a school building and every minute of the school day. Teachers whose Makerspace is in a few cardboard boxes are doing brilliant work. Making across the curriculum means students as novelists, mathematicians, historians, composers, artists, engineers—rather than being the recipients of instruction.[3]

If we truly want our students to apply their learning and create new knowledge and ideas, we need to ensure students have opportunities to practice this kind of learning throughout the day and across disciplines. The idea of "build it and they will come" does not apply to education. The shift in our thinking must focus on *what learning truly can be*, not what it has been.

SCHOOL VERSUS LEARNING

In 2014, I wrote a blog post titled "School vs. Learning" that challenged the idea of "traditional school" and how people actually learn. Here were some of the ideas I shared:

- *School promotes starting by looking for answers. Learning promotes starting with questions.*

- *School is about consuming. Learning is about creating.*

- *School is about finding information on something prescribed for you. Learning is about exploring your passions and interests.*

- *School teaches compliance. Learning is about challenging perceived norms.*

- *School is scheduled at certain times. Learning can happen any time, all of the time.*

- *School often isolates. Learning is often social.*

- *School is standardized. Learning is personal.*

- *School teaches us to obtain information from certain people. Learning promotes that everyone is a teacher, and everyone is a learner.*

- *School is about giving you information. Learning is about making your own connections.*

- *School is sequential. Learning is random and non-linear.*

- *School promotes surface-level thinking. Learning is about deep exploration.*[4]

I know the statements above are not one hundred percent true on either side of the spectrum, but what if you combined the statements to make something new? Would schools become a place that is truly developing learners who are flexible and agile in a world that is constantly changing? For example, take the statement:

School promotes starting by looking for answers. Learning promotes starting with questions.

… and change it to this:

School promotes developing your own questions and finding answers.

Imagine what school would look like if we really focused on empowering learners.

School vs Learning by George Couros

SCHOOL
- promotes starting by looking for answers
- is about consuming
- is about finding information on something prescribed for you
- teaches compliance
- is scheduled at certain times
- often isolates
- is standardized
- teaches us to obtain information from certain people
- is about giving you information
- is sequential ABCDE
- promotes surface-level thinking

@gcouros   bit.ly/schoolvslearning

LEARNING
- promotes starting with questions
- is about creating
- is about exploring your passions and interests
- is about challenging perceived norms
- can happen any time, all of the time
- is often social
- is personal
- promotes that everyone is a teacher and everyone is a learner
- is about making your own connections
- is random and non-linear
- is about deep exploration

@sylviaduckworth

(Sylvia Duckworth created this image to summarize the contrasted ideas nicely.[5])

THE WORLD ~~OUR KIDS~~ WE LIVE IN

If we want to truly create the opportunities for *learning* as described in the statements above, we must keep in mind that a culture of compliance will not foster the environments we want for students or educators. Demanding compliance will not effectively prepare learners for being productive citizens today, nor in their futures.

One statement that drives me insane is, "We need to prepare kids for the world that they live in." We *all* actually live in the same world. We *all* need to develop the skills and mindsets that will help us thrive, not only in the classroom but also in our lives beyond the school walls. Empowering students to succeed in school *and* life—means that we pay attention to the skills companies are seeking. In Chapter 2, I mentioned Thomas Friedman's article "How to Get a Job at Google."[6] In it, he highlighted five hiring attributes that the company desires in its employees. "Compliance" isn't listed. Take a look at what is:

1. **Cognitive Ability:** "The ability to process on the fly."

2. **Leadership:** Emergent leadership versus traditional leadership. As a leader, do you recognize the times when you need to relinquish power?

3. **Humility:** The ability to say, "I don't know," and be able to step back and embrace better ideas.

4. **Ownership:** Understanding that an organizational problem is also *your* problem, and working together to solve it is crucial.

5. **Expertise:** This is listed as the least important attribute, because thinking you already know the answer can keep you from exploring new options.

Friedman closes with a note to which schools should pay close attention: "In an age when innovation is increasingly a group endeavor, it [Google] also cares about a lot of soft skills—leadership, humility, collaboration, adaptability, and loving to learn and re-learn. This will be true no matter where you go to work."

 EMPOWERING STUDENTS TO SUCCEED IN SCHOOL AND LIFE—MEANS THAT WE PAY ATTENTION TO THE SKILLS COMPANIES ARE SEEKING.

MOVING FORWARD

As we move forward in education and consider these characteristics that Google looks for, and the world expects, creating a culture of compliance or engagement is simply not enough—and may actually be detrimental. Our school communities need to ensure these "soft skills" are valued and become the norm, not the exception. Only then will both students and staff feel empowered to learn and free to take risks that will help our schools move forward.

QUESTIONS FOR DISCUSSION

1. How do we create learning opportunities and experiences for students and staff that focus on empowerment, as opposed to engagement?

2. What new statements would you create with the "School vs. Learning" image? Are they on one side of the spectrum, or are these statements closer to the middle?

3. How do we create classrooms and schools where students and voices are not only heard but needed?

NOTES

1. Seth Godin, "Stop Stealing Dreams," YouTube video, 16:57, October 16, 2012, https://www.youtube.com/watch?v=sXpbONjV1Jc.

2. Images used with permission: Bill Ferriter, @PlugUsIn, http://blog.williamferriter.com.

3. Gary Stager, "Gary Stager: The Best 'Makerspace' Is Between Your Ears," *American School Board Journal* (June 2015): 58.

4. George Couros, "School Vs. Learning," *The Principal of Change: Stories of Leading and Learning* (blog), December 27, 2014, http://georgecouros.ca/blog/archives/4974.

5. Image used with permission: Sylvia Duckworth (@sylviaduckworth), https://www.flickr.com/photos/15664662@N02/.

6. Thomas Friedman, "How to Get a Job at Google," *The New York Times*, February 22, 2014, http://www.nytimes.com/2014/02/23/opinion/sunday/friedman-how-to-get-a-job-at-google.html?_r=0.

CHAPTER 7
CREATING A SHARED VISION

Big thinking precedes great
achievement.

−Wilferd Peterson

Walking through a recruitment fair, I noticed a sign that was meant to attract visionary educators to the school district. It read, "Acme School District… A great place to work." (To avoid incriminating anyone, I've changed the school district's name.)

Wow. Not very compelling. This sign told me nothing about the school district or who it serves. If the draw was supposed to be that it is "a great place to work," well, *any* organization or retail company might post that on its website. Even if the uninspiring statement is true, it still leaves us wondering about the district's priorities and how educators attend to the needs of stakeholders.

Our vision for what education can look like today should be compelling not only to our students but also to teachers, leaders, and the greater community—and it has to be better than being "a great place to work." But before we decide how best to communicate our vision, we have to establish one; we have to articulate the desired characteristics of our learners and the optimal learning environment. It's important to note, too, that *how* we go about creating a school or district's vision and mission statements will determine, in large part, whether it compels people to participate in making it a reality.

The people who help set the vision and mission are the most likely to embrace it. If an organization wants to define its vision and mission on a weekend retreat, but invites only administrators, then only the administrators are going to be truly excited about it. However, if the administration includes the rest of the staff in the vision creation process, it's more likely that everyone will jump on board with it. Why? It goes back to the notion of moving from *compliance and engagement* to *empowerment.* To truly be empowered, people need both ownership and autonomy. To move forward in education—to create a vision for education that then comes to life—we must take more than a top-down or bottom-up approach; we will need all hands on deck.

A NEW VISION

In 2011, the leaders at Parkland School Division, a district of twenty-two schools located west of Edmonton, Alberta, Canada, recognized the need for a shift in their thinking. Part of that shift began with involving the entire community in the process of developing a new *vision and mission* for learning. In addition to staff and students, the leaders consulted with parents and business leaders to not only *engage* them in the process but also empower them. Not everyone could attend the meetings, of course. With a school community of 10,000 students, it is hard to bring everyone together face-to-face, but technology ensured that everyone had the opportunity to share their thoughts. Individuals and groups offered input on what they saw as necessary for students—both for the present and for their future. Words like *creativity*, *innovation*, and *exploration* came up repeatedly; the word *compliance* did not.

Part of the process included using prompts to get people thinking differently. Rather than serving as a road map, these prompts opened people's minds to discuss what education could really look like. For example, the image below from Krissy Venosdale[1] provides a great example of the shifts that are possible in education. Questions such as *What is imperative? What is great? What is missing?* helped facilitate a

conversation that allowed all stakeholders to think about the possibilities for education and create a new vision for their community schools.

After a significant amount of effort and hours spent compiling input from such a diverse group, a new vision was created:

Parkland School Division is a place where exploration, creativity, and imagination make learning exciting and where all learners aspire to reach their dreams.

Created through the same process, the mission explains how the vision will become a reality:

Our purpose is to prepare, engage, and inspire our students to be their best in a quickly changing global community.

Notice that the purposeful wording of the vision statement uses the term "learners" instead "students." Parkland School Division, along with many forward-thinking educational organizations around the world, recognize that learning—at all levels—is paramount to creating an innovative culture in schools. If we want innovative students, we need to be innovative leaders and educators. If we want to create a culture of innovation, we must first focus on furthering our own learning and growth.

What I love most about Parkland School Division's vision is its lack of *generic-ness*; it is unique to the community it serves. It also makes the strong statement that anyone who is part of the school division is encouraged to *"reach their dreams."* The fact that I am writing this book is an example of how this particular school district supports anyone with great aspirations, not just students, who is willing to embrace the identity of a learner. And the powerful, clear vision and mission statements are much more compelling for all stakeholders than, "A great place to work!"

ACTION REQUIRED

Vision without execution is hallucination.

— Thomas Edison

A vision statement should be clear and direct enough to memorize. It is also important that it can connect with each and every person in the organization. "Systems thinking" is a crucial component of creating a culture shift, but if we do not understand (or can't quickly explain) how the larger vision translates into the classroom and learning, we have created nothing but words. "Systems thinking" doesn't

IF WE WANT TO CREATE A CULTURE OF INNOVATION, WE MUST FIRST FOCUS ON FURTHERING OUR OWN LEARNING AND GROWTH.

mean much if we don't have "systems doing." To ensure that the vision is attained, we must break down the mission into small, achievable steps for the individuals within our school system. Each step achieved toward the end goal helps to build confidence and competence along the way. And when the individuals are successful, the entire organization benefits.

8 THINGS TO LOOK FOR IN TODAY'S CLASSROOM

As you determine which actions will help achieve your school or district's vision, it will be helpful to keep in mind the characteristics of learning environments that inspire innovative thinking. Through my own research and study, I've noticed that organizations that are successful at executing their vision have or encourage the following things daily in learning.

1. **Voice**—Learning is social, and co-constructing knowledge empowers learners. Students should have the opportunity to learn from others and to share their learning with others. In our world today, there are many opportunities to share one's voice. As we empower students to speak up, we must teach them to use their voices effectively. If left to figure it out on their own, they will definitely struggle.

2. **Choice**—Choice concerns both how students learn and what they learn. How do they further learning and develop expertise in *their* areas of interest? I did poorly throughout the first few years of

university. In my final few years, my grades significantly improved. What was the difference? I had choice in my classes and actually cared about what I was learning. Providing choice allows students to build on strengths and interests to make learning relevant and fulfilling.

3. **Time for Reflection**—Classrooms are extremely busy places. I understand why many teachers feel they must rush through the curriculum and struggle to fit everything in. To allow for deeper learning, taking the time to connect and reflect allows learners a better opportunity to really think about and understand what they have learned. As discussed earlier, DEAR time should be an opportunity not only for reading but to also "Drop Everything And Reflect." John Dewey is quoted as having said, "We do not learn from experience; we learn from reflecting on experience." Reflection time should not be an optional component of the classroom or even done on "your own time." It should be a regular part of both student and educator practice.

4. **Opportunities for Innovation**—I visited Greystone Centennial Middle School during its "Innovation Week" and met students who had created a hovercraft using things that they had around the house. (I'm not kidding.) They were able to guide it around the gym, and it could carry people from place to place. These students were in grade *eight*.

   When I asked the students about their passion project, they told me that they had seen a video of something similar on YouTube. They took that idea and added a few elements they felt were missing. In other words, they made it new and better. It is important that "innovation" does not become an event for our students but the norm. It is imperative to create ongoing opportunities in all areas where students are encouraged and provided time to develop and pursue innovative ideas.

5. **Critical Thinkers**—The "factory model" of education forced

students to be compliant and basically do "as they were told." Compliance doesn't help children remember lessons long term, but it can create an attitude that follows them well into adulthood.

One of my best friends, and my first admin partner, asked me to never allow him to go out on his own with his ideas without questioning them and sharing my thoughts. His reason? He wanted the best ideas, not just his ideas. He wanted me to ask questions and challenge ideas to ensure they were successful. It was not his ego that led him but his desire to see his staff and students flourish. I have learned to ask the same of the people I work with. Although spirited conversations may spark as a result, thinking critically and asking questions are good practices for all organizations.

Critical thinking is also important because we live in a world where information is abundant—something that is both a benefit and detriment. Having so many ideas and facts at their fingertips

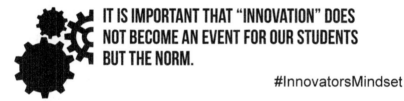

IT IS IMPORTANT THAT "INNOVATION" DOES NOT BECOME AN EVENT FOR OUR STUDENTS BUT THE NORM.

#InnovatorsMindset

is helpful for students—as long as they understand how to discern truth from fiction and know why it's important to consider the source of the information. That's why author and blogger Howard Rheingold emphasizes the importance of "crap detection." He explains, "It's up to you to sort the accurate bits from the misinfo, disinfo, spam, scams, urban legends, and hoaxes. 'Crap detection,' as Hemingway called it half a century ago, is more important than ever before."[2]

We need to teach students to respectfully ask questions and empower them to challenge the ideas of others to help all move forward, not to challenge simply for the sake of it.

6. **Problem Solvers/Finders**—As discussed earlier, it is important to develop a generation of not only problem "solvers" but also problem "finders." Principal Megan Howard shared a wonderful story with me about how one of her grade six students "found" a problem: children lost pieces of their school uniforms. The student suggested using QR codes to reunite kids with their lost belongings. This was done through the school's "Capstone Project," where students find problems that impact their community and have a certain time frame to do research and solve them. More and more schools are creating these types of opportunities for their students. These student-led projects often focus on empowering kids to make an impact on the world right now. Let's start asking kids to find problems and give them a sense of purpose in solving something authentic.

7. **Self-Assessment**—I have never heard a teacher say, "I can't wait until we get to write report cards!" When you think about who is doing the work, often it's teachers who are spending countless hours collecting evidence to show others what our students know and can do. If you can write in a report card that a student can do something in October but they can't do it in January, is that report card still relevant? Teaching students how to assess themselves, rather than just do it for them, provides them another opportunity for reflection. And they will take ownership of their learning.

   I think we spend too much time documenting what students know and not enough time empowering them to invest in their own learning and helping them understand their strengths and areas of growth. Portfolios are a great way for learners to share their knowledge and document the learning process. Looking back helps students develop their own understanding of where they have been, where they are, and where they are going.

8. **Connected Learning**—When I first started teaching, I really struggled with science. It was a subject that challenged me as a

learner, and becoming a teacher didn't change that. If I were in the classroom today, I still wouldn't be the best person to teach science, but a scientist might be. And that's where connected learning comes in. Today, we can use Skype, FaceTime, Google Hangouts, and the like to connect with experts, from any number of fields and industries, who are willing to share their knowledge. Of course, connection does not only have to be via technology; we can also bring in local experts to talk to students. Teachers can design and activate powerful learning experiences for students to engage with content experts and apply their learning to create new knowledge and ideas. Technology provides access to people we could not even imagine being a part of our classroom even ten years ago.

Another way we can connect is through social media, which makes it possible for students to get feedback from others. Teachers, like grade four Kelli Holden (@kholden), have their students share their thoughts and tap into expertise from people around the world. I've even taken part in a "blog launch" party where the students wrote their own posts and shared them online.

Think about it: From whom would you rather learn about space? An astronaut or a teacher? The answer seems obvious. We want to learn from the experts. Since that's true, let's take advantage of technology and facilitate those connections. More importantly, let's teach students to facilitate these powerful learning opportunities themselves.

VISION TO REALITY

In an earlier chapter, I talked about remixing concepts from others and adapting them to suit our needs. After I wrote a blog post in 2015 about these eight characteristics,[3] Sylvia Duckworth created a graphic based on what I shared.[4] Aside from being very creative with the content, the image was helpful for many visual learners.

Images often spark ideas—especially when we share them. And that's what happened when the Parkland School Division leadership team took Sylvia's image and discussed it with the division's student advisory group. Students were asked what they thought about the graphic and were encouraged to talk about it with their teachers. The conversations that were sparked between the students and educators focused on how (or if) these eight things were being achieved in the classroom. What I found incredibly valuable about this process of sparking ideas through printed words, images, and discussion was the chance to *empower* students to share their learning with their teachers and, ultimately, impact the type of education and learning experiences in which they engaged.

Again, these "eight things" aren't meant to be a road map for what classrooms should look like but to spark ideas and innovation of what could be. Far too often, schools spend a lot of time creating a vision for students in which they have little input. Instead, when educators create

8 Things to Look for in Today's Classroom
by George Couros

1 VOICE
★ Students should learn from others and then share their learning.

2 CHOICE
★ STRENGTH-BASED LEARNING
★ Give students a choice.

3 TIME FOR REFLECTION
★ EVERYONE (teachers, admin, students) should write and reflect on what is being learned.

8 CONNECTED LEARNING
★ Bring experts into your class via social media and video-conferencing.

CLASSROOMS need to be LEARNER-FOCUSSED

4 OPPORTUNITIES for INNOVATION
★ Example: Build a hovercraft from a YouTube video! (yes, it can be done!)

7 SELF-ASSESSMENT
★ Important that students know how to do this.
★ Use portfolios.

6 PROBLEM SOLVERS/FINDERS
★ Give students tough challenges and let them find innovative solutions.

5 CRITICAL THINKERS
★ Ask questions and challenge what you see.

bit.ly/gcouros8

@sylviaduckworth

IN A PLACE WHERE EVERY LEARNER IS ENCOURAGED TO REACH HIS OR HER DREAMS, THESE "WHAT IFS" CAN BECOME REALITY.

opportunities to listen and honor student voices, they can co-construct relevant and authentic learning experiences and make the vision a reality.

WHAT IF?

A process that I have found very helpful in creating a new vision for schools and developing a strategy to get there is something I call "What if?" This is a process meant to help you dream big and to figure out what is important for you and your educational organization as you move forward. Here are some of my "What ifs":

What if we believed that everything that we had to make great schools was already within our organization, and we just needed to develop and share it?

What if schools operated as if we should all be "learners," as opposed to students being the only learners?

What if we promoted "risk-taking" to our staff and students and modeled it openly as administrators?

What if we hired people who did not look at teaching as a "career" but as a "passion"?

What if everyone in our organization, not just our students, was encouraged to pursue his or her dreams?

What if we focused on connecting and learning, both globally and locally?

What if people were always our first focus, as opposed to "stuff"?

What if we recognized and built on learners' strengths?

What if we empowered students to make a difference in the world today *and* in the future?

MOVING FORWARD

The future belongs to those who see possibilities before they become obvious.

—John Scully[5]

In a place where *every* learner is encouraged to reach his or her dreams, these "what ifs" can become reality. How we create opportunities and remove barriers moving forward is crucial. My parents did not come to Canada to recreate what they already had somewhere else. They came to this country to create something better for themselves and their family. Dreaming is important, but until we create the conditions where innovation in education flourishes, those dreams will not become reality.

QUESTIONS FOR DISCUSSION

1. How do you involve the greater community into creating an inspiring vision for learning in your school or organization?

2. Does your vision (individually and organizationally) reflect the powerful learning opportunities that are available today? Is it compelling and empowering to educators?

3. What are the small steps along the way that you will need to make the vision reality?

NOTES

1. Image used with permission: Krissy Venosdale (@venspired), "A Tale of Two Classrooms," *Venspired.com* May 30, 2012, http://venspired.com/a-tale-of-two-classrooms/.

2. Howard Rheingold, "Crap Detection 101," *City Brights: Howard Rheingold* (blog), SFGate, June 30, 2009, http://blog.sfgate.com/rheingold/2009/06/30/crap-detection-101/.

3. George Couros, "8 Things to Look for in Today's Classroom," *The Principal of Change: Stories of Leading and Learning* (blog), January 8, 2013, http://georgecouros.ca/blog/archives/3586.

4. Image used with permission: Sylvia Duckworth (@sylviaduckworth), https://www.flickr.com/photos/15664662@N02/.

5. John Scully, *Moonshot! Game-Changing Strategies to Build Billion-Dollar Businesses* (New York: RosettaBooks, 2014).

PART III:
UNLEASHING TALENT

Up to this point, we've focused on defining innovation and laying the groundwork necessary for a culture where innovative thinking becomes the norm in our schools. To recap: Innovation is a mindset—a way of thinking—that creates something new and better. By developing trust and collaborating with your community, you can empower educators and learners to take risks that move our schools forward.

In the next few chapters, we'll focus on how to lead in such a way that you unleash people's talent. My hope is you will see that, while it's important to understand what innovation is, book knowledge isn't enough, and directing with a top-down mentality isn't effective. I truly believe that, in educational leadership, you will be more successful when you demonstrate to the people you serve that innovation isn't a command, but is something you are willing to do with your team. It starts by changing ourselves. To help move others forward, we must first look in the mirror at our actions and, sometimes, inaction. Do that, and you'll unleash their talent and create a culture where innovation flourishes.

CHAPTER 8
STRENGTHS-BASED LEADERSHIP

When we build on our strengths and daily successes–instead of focusing on failures–we simply learn more.

-Tom Rath[1]

Success is achieved by developing our strengths, not by eliminating our weaknesses.

-Marilyn vos Savant[2]

onsider this common educational practice: A student struggles in math, so to help him achieve success in the discipline, the teacher sends him home with extra practice work. The teacher may even recommend an extra math class in lieu of electives. What often happens in such situations is that the student does not improve in math but learns to hate it and school.

Remember the *what ifs* from the previous chapter? Well, what if we stopped operating on a deficit model that focuses on a learner's weaknesses and started operating on a strengths-based model that builds on the learner's strengths? If we are going to empower our students, we must help them find what they love and create learning experiences that encourage them to develop their strengths.

So if students excel in writing, let's create more opportunities for them to write. If they are excited about science, let's look for ways to provide opportunities for them to explore that passion. Imagine what education would look like if we did that!

Unfortunately, we dangle students' interests in front of them like a carrot. We say, "You can only do what you love when you finish that which you hate." As a beginning teacher, rather than encourage a student's enjoyment of physical education, I would threaten to keep them out of P.E. class if they did not finish their "work" in another subject area. It wasn't a helpful approach, but it was what I experienced as a student and, in turn, thought it was what I was supposed to do to my students. As a result, my students often begrudgingly finished their

AN ENVIRONMENT WHERE THE MESSAGE IS ALWAYS "WE ARE NOT GOOD ENOUGH" CAN BE DEMORALIZING AND COUNTERPRODUCTIVE FOR ALL STAKEHOLDERS.

assignments (compliance model), but the incident always diminished the relationship between the student and myself. How could it not?

Let me clarify that focusing on strengths does not equate to ignoring areas of weakness. To the contrary, a strengths-based model can actually encourage students to improve in their weaker areas. Remember: success builds competence and confidence. So if school is a place where students are put into situations in which they are likely to feel successful, they develop confidence. By continually offering opportunities that stretch students in their strengths, they improve their learning skills, as well as their belief in themselves. Each challenge that students overcome helps them understand that, while some subjects may come more easily to them than others, they *can* learn and it can be fun! When teachers then harness the power of the child's newly developed growth mindset, they can help them improve in even those more challenging subjects.

LEADING FOR BETTER TEACHING—AND BETTER LEARNING

Teachers often design classroom experiences that mimic the school culture and the learning opportunities they've experienced. So when teachers are part of a culture that is built on a deficit model, that mentality often manifests itself in the classroom. One example of this is the way testing data is used to identify and address areas of weakness. This practice leaves a lot of educators feeling demoralized in their work.

Recently, I read an article in the *Toronto Sun* titled "Literacy Rates up but Students still Struggling with Math."[3] The piece about Canada's Ontario province focused entirely on math. Not one sentence celebrated the province's improvement in literacy. The focus was, instead, on how math instruction and learning were not up to par. Should Ontario just ignore math scores and adopt the "you win some, you lose some" mentality? Absolutely not. Neither should its complete focus be on improving declining math results. Yet we continue to play this game of educational "whack-a-mole," where one problem pops up and we focus on that until the next issue arises.

We cannot forgo a focus on our strengths for the sake of only emphasizing the areas where we struggle. But that's what happens time and again. The deficit model compels administrators and educators to overcompensate in the areas that need to be "fixed." When that occurs, all the great things that are already happening are quickly forgotten. The bottom line is: an environment where the message is always "we are not good enough" can be demoralizing and counterproductive for all stakeholders.

Author and human behavior researcher Tom Rath notes in his book, *Strengths Finder 2.0*, that, "[P]eople who do have the opportunity to focus on their strengths every day are *six times as likely to be engaged in their jobs* and more than *three times as likely to report having an excellent quality of life in general*."[4] Clearly we need to make sure our educators and students have ample opportunity to explore and practice in areas which they thrive.

But that doesn't means we, as leaders, should simply step back and leave growth to chance. In fact, Rath's research found that people were far more engaged in their work when managers focused on their employees' strengths—rather than just assuming they would continue to grow in those areas. He notes:

> *In 2005, we explored what happens when managers primarily focus on employees' strengths, primarily focus on employees' weakness, or ignore employees. What we found completely redefined my perspective about how easy it may be to decrease the active disengagement, or extreme negativity, that runs rampant in organizations.* [5]

If your manager primarily:	The chances of you being actively disengaged are:
Ignores you	40%
Focuses on your weaknesses	22%
Focuses on your strengths	1%

As you can see from the results above, having a manager who ignores you is even more detrimental than having a manager who primarily focuses on your weaknesses. Perhaps most surprising is the degree to which having a manager who focuses on your strengths decreases the odds of you being miserable on the job. It appears that the epidemic of active disengagement we see in workplaces every day could be a curable disease, if we can help the people around us develop their strengths.

GREAT LEADERS PRACTICE BALANCING TRUST AND AUTONOMY WHILE PROVIDING STRONG MENTORSHIP.

#InnovatorsMindset

What really resonated with me from this point was how *ignoring* an employee had a more negative effect than focusing on his or her weaknesses. I often hear educators talk about how their leadership stays out of their way. Although I understand (and teach) that trust and autonomy are essential to motivation, there is a larger purpose to what we, as a group of individuals, do in schools. As teachers and leaders, we are stronger and more effective when we work together and push one another to grow. If we are to believe Rath's research (and I do), simply "leaving people alone" is not the best approach.

Great leaders practice balancing trust and autonomy while providing strong mentorship. Leading does not necessarily mean telling people what to do or how to do it. Rather, it often requires pushing others' thinking and abilities by asking questions and challenging perceptions without micro-managing.

We only get better when we find those who truly elevate us. Look for mentors who will push you to come up with better and brighter ideas and be that person for your followers. Leaders are meant to unleash talent by bringing their people's strengths to life, not ignoring them.

To create a culture where innovation flourishes, we have to realize that, in many cases, we already have everything we need; we just need to figure out how to tap into it.

THE WRONG APPROACH

In my first year as a principal, I really wanted to support our students in blogging. To me, that meant we, as educators and leaders, needed to blog as well. In my ignorance, I thought I could inspire people by really pounding home the message that we were behind in this area and that the only way we could get better was by doing it ourselves. I did exactly what I hate seeing done to our students: I hoped that my staff would use their own time to focus on an area of weakness. Although some staff reluctantly did so, I quickly figured out that this approach was not effective in creating the learning culture I desired.

What did work was spending time with people one-on-one and looking at their strengths in teaching. I made a point of emphasizing and articulating the areas in which they excelled. My hope was that, by focusing on each individual's strengths, our school could move forward in a number of areas, not just blogging. Instead of saying, "We need to blog because we are so far behind in this area for our students," I said, "I saw that you did these things very well, and it would be so beneficial for all staff to learn from this expertise. Would you consider sitting down with me and blogging about it?" Ultimately, the strengths were the first focus to help us move forward, and it was an opportunity to validate the great things that were already happening in our schools.

It takes far less energy to move from first-rate performance to excellence than it does to move from incompetence to mediocrity.

—Peter Drucker[6]

A CUSTOM FIT

Kelly Wilkins, deputy superintendent of Parkland School Division, is a master of tapping into the strengths of others. One of my first encounters with her was as a teacher on her staff where she was principal. Before I even worked one day for her, I knew she had a different approach to leadership. In the hiring process, the job title was quite open-ended (middle school teacher, grade level yet to be determined), which allowed her some flexibility in hiring. I had spent the first part of my career teaching elementary students and the second part teaching high school students; I didn't have much experience at all with the middle school level. That being said, she noticed things on my résumé and portfolio that were unique and created a position tailored to my strengths, rather than to a specific position. One superintendent I worked with said, "We do not fit people into jobs. We find the best people and fit the jobs to them." Kelly has embodied this idea her entire career, and that is why she is known in our district as a developer of leaders. Although I still taught certain subjects and grades that were required, there were parts of the position that were tailored to my knowledge of how to effectively use technology. Kelly's willingness to be innovative inside the box helped create an opportunity for me—which, in turn, empowered me to do the same for my students.

In your own school or organization, you may notice that, when one person excels in a position or a school creates amazing results, you often see that exact same position replicated again and again in other organizations, but the results don't measure up. Why is this? Because "titles" do not create results; people do. Building upon the strengths of your people ensures that you get more out of them, not less.

BUILD EACH OTHER UP TO BUILD SOMETHING TOGETHER

As I started this new middle school position (which actually never had a title), one of my roles was to help integrate technology into learning. In my previous roles, I had taught students how to use technology in computer courses. In this role, I would teach students to use technology to improve and accelerate learning in other subjects, such as English and history. As my principal, Kelly was transparent about her goals and what she wanted me to do, and she empowered me to lead in a way that I felt would work best.

Initially, I was scheduled for a forty-minute block with each classroom during the week. I would sometimes get two sessions in a row with a classroom, but my time was spread equally within the school amongst teachers. Something about the schedule did not seem right to me, but, being new to the school, I did not want to rock the boat. However, what I learned early on about Kelly was that she kept her focus on what was best for kids. With that in mind, I told her I thought the schedule needed to allow for us to go deeper into the learning with technology, as opposed to having short amounts of exposure. I suggested that it would be better to be with one classroom for at least a week, or maybe two weeks, to create opportunities that could allow for deeper learning for both the students and staff that I served. I also explained that it would be more beneficial if we focused on projects as opposed to lessons. After listening to my concerns, she said, "I hired you as the expert in this area. You do whatever you think is best."

Kelly had wanted people to try new things with the vision of doing "what is best for kids" always out in the forefront. If we could do something different that was *better* for our students, then we needed to explore that. She showed, by her own example, that she was willing to take risks in her own practice as well. This is a crucial element of leadership. People will not feel comfortable taking risks in an organization unless leaders are willing to take risks themselves, share the things they are doing, and try to improve themselves. Kelly modeled this by creating environments where she pushed people to think of new and better solutions, while never micro-managing or pushing for perfection.

Learning is messy, and we have to be comfortable with risk, failure, growth, and revision. Once people see leaders take risks, they are more likely to try their own ideas and stretch themselves—and their students. Giving people license to take risks by tapping into their abilities helps create a space where innovative ideas and learning flourish.

> Instead of wondering if someone is smart, they wonder in what way that person is smart.
>
> –Liz Wiseman et al.[7]

YOUR DREAM JOB

I learned a lot from Kelly and am thankful that I still have the opportunity to do so today. As someone who strives to bring out the best in people, she has taught me a lot about tapping into others' strengths and giving them the chance to shape their own opportunities. As Liz Wiseman and Greg McKeown share in the book *Multipliers*, "Finding someone's native genius is the key that unlocks discretionary effort. It propels people to go beyond what is required and offer their full intelligence."[8] Sometimes, to find out what people's strengths are, all you have to do is ask.

When I became a principal, I sent out an email each year as we began the staffing process. It read, "As we are currently undergoing staffing, we were wondering if you could describe your dream position next year, what would it be?"

Obviously, there was only so much we could do if you said you wanted to be an astronaut or a reality TV personality. But in the context of the school, we wondered what opportunities we could create.

The important thing about asking this question was, for starters, asking the question. We could not guarantee we could create the job that a teacher wanted. But unless we encouraged people to share what they dreamed of doing, how would we know? I remember one elementary school teacher responding that, although he loved working with grade five students, he would really like to work with kindergarten or grade one students. The crazy thing was we had a grade one teacher

 SOMETIMES, PEOPLE ARE AFRAID TO SHARE WHAT THEY WANT BECAUSE THEY DON'T KNOW THAT GETTING IT IS EVEN A POSSIBILITY.

#InnovatorsMindset

who wanted to work with our older students. A simple swap was made. Both teachers were amazing in their new classrooms and unbelievably grateful for the opportunity.

Another teacher shared that he loved teaching one particular subject and wasn't too passionate about the one that he was asked to teach in the current school year. He loved working with students but knew he was more effective when he was passionate about the subjects he taught. With a couple of adjustments, he was placed in an area where he thought he would excel; and he was amazing.

I also remember a grade two teacher's response that affirmed the need to ask about my staff's desires. She wrote, "My dream job is teaching grade two, and I get to live it every single day. But I just want to tell you how much I appreciate you asking in the first place."

Giving people the chance to try something new or pursue something they love is not something we should only value for our students but also for our staff. Sometimes, people are afraid to share what they want because they don't know that getting it is even a possibility. The way my fellow administrators and I saw it was that if we can move people into positions where they feel passionate about what they are doing, they are more likely to be successful as individuals, elevating the organization as a whole. And it continually surprised me that we were very often able to accommodate their requests.

A colleague of mine and current principal for Parkland School Division, Carolyn Jensen, shared with me her belief that, as leaders, we should not limit the question to *this* year but also help create opportunities for our team member's future. She says:

> Another important question is "Where do you see your career in the next three to five years?" Knowing who may be interested in moving into leadership is valuable info to have when District Office is looking for people for committee work...professional development and collegial connections can be made as teachers begin to expand their practice. Just as we see teachers help students blossom by taking a personal interest in them and bringing in special activities or items, teachers will grow professionally when their administrators take a personal interest in their careers. When teachers feel cared for, just like students, it goes a long way toward creating a great school culture.

Carolyn reminds me and others that when we show a genuine interest in those whom we serve and go out of our way to help them become successful in areas about which they are passionate, they are more likely to go above and beyond what is expected.

THE IMPORTANCE OF OWNERSHIP

Once you have a focus on strengths-based leadership, it is crucial to empower your staff and give them ownership in leading the direction of your school or organization. A few years ago, while working with a new staff, I proposed that we could lead the professional learning opportunities within our own school. We did not seek outside experts because we had the expertise within the building. As the principal, I suggested that we limit our focus to three areas for the year. Based on the feedback of my staff, they actually added a fourth focus area to include: technology integration, inclusion, critical thinking, and citizenship and social responsibility. Each of these priorities was to be led by a team created within the school. My only stipulation was that staff members join a team in which they were strong or had an interest. Rather than joining a team with a focus in an area where they felt they needed to improve, I wanted them to follow their passions. I believed that the more interested they were in the topic, the better the learning would be for the entire staff.

I asked them to develop the goals for each team and define the measures of success. My thought was that they, as the experts, would understand what success looks like and be able to set the guidelines for the school. As the principal, I oversaw the plan (I was also on one of the teams as an equal member, not a boss, which was crucial to the success), but I knew that, if we were going to grow as a staff and implement some new initiatives, my staff needed to feel they had real ownership in both the process and the outcomes. That's the difference between achieving "our goals" as opposed to "my goals."

Exploring our strengths and passions, along with sharing and learning from one another, provided some of the most innovative and empowering professional development that I had ever been a part of. Each group came up with many different ways to implement their ideas and improve learning for both students and the staff. While we supported and learned from one another, we also pushed each other to be better. The teachers and staff started to see each other as experts and valued their contribution and expertise. An added benefit of this experience was that teachers modeled the group- and student-led approach in their classrooms. We were learning about different aspects of our job and, at the same time, discovering ways to be more effective in creating powerful learning opportunities.

MOVING FORWARD

Focusing on individuals' strengths that contribute to the vision of the school helps to move us from pockets of innovation to a culture where innovation flourishes. When each individual is recognized for his or her own unique qualities and how those strengths support the overall vision of learning for our school, we can truly transform our schools. By focusing on strengths first and building from there, as opposed to working from a deficit model that focuses only on where we need improvements, we create an environment where people feel they have a purpose in their classrooms and for the entire school. This is how to encourage that shift from classroom teacher to school teacher that we discussed in Chapter 4.

As you look to change and improve your school, district, or division, realize that everything you need may already exist within your organization. Your job is to unleash the talents of your staff members. Start by modeling the behaviors you want—collaborating, taking risks, valuing, and being willing to learn from those on your team or in your class.

As stated previously in this book, relationships are the most important element of schools. When you consistently start conversation with, "Here is where we need to improve" or tell people how the work has to be done, you build a culture of compliance and leave people wondering where they add value. If you are new to an organization (or have even been there for a while), my best advice is to sit back, wait a bit, and ensure that you are able to identify where people shine. Tap into those strengths and use them to move forward.

Do we really think someone will be innovative in an area they hate?

QUESTIONS FOR DISCUSSION

1. What are the current strengths of your organization and how do you continue to move them forward?

2. What are the strengths of the individuals you serve and how have you put them into situations where these strengths will flourish?

3. How do you find the balance between "mentoring" and "micro-managing" to ensure people feel supported and comfortable taking risks?

NOTES

1. Tom Rath, *Strengths Based Leadership: Great Leaders, Teams, and Why People Follow* (New York: Gallup Press, 2008).

2. Marilyn vos Savant, "Developing Your Strengths," *Parade*, October 31, 2014.

3. Maryam Shah, "Literacy Rates Up but Students Still Struggling with Math," *Toronto Sun*, August 27, 2014, http://www.torontosun.com/2014/08/27/literacy-rates-up-but-students-still-struggling-with-math.

4. Tom Rath, *Strengths Finder 2.0* (New York: Gallup Press, 2007), iii.

5. *Ibid.*, iv.

6. Peter F. Drucker, *The Practice of Management* (New York: Harper & Row, 1954).

7. Liz Wiseman, Lois N. Allen, and Elise Foster, *The Multiplier Effect: Tapping the Genius Inside Our Schools* (Thousand Oaks, CA: Corwin, 2013), 9.

8. Liz Wiseman with Greg McKeown, *Multipliers: How the Best Leaders Make Everyone Smarter* (New York: HarperCollins, 2010), 31.

CHAPTER 9
POWERFUL LEARNING FIRST, TECHNOLOGY SECOND

A point of view can be a dangerous luxury when substituted for insight and understanding.

–Marshal McLuhan[1]

We were about to leave on a trip when I noticed my brother tweeted out a sweet video of my niece, Bea. Never missing a chance to see what my lovely nephews and nieces are up to, I immediately watched and was blown away by what she was doing. After seeing a tutorial video about how to apply makeup, she had decided to make her own. She carefully showed different color choices and went through how to apply eye shadow, lip liner, mascara, and blush (I needed my own tutorial to learn what these things were!). She was four years old at the time.

Other than being utterly adorable (I am totally biased, but, seriously, check out "Bea's Makeup Tutorial" on YouTube[2]), what really struck me about this video is how, before children even walk into a school, they have both the opportunity to learn from and teach others.

Technology invites us to move from *engaged to empowered*. It provides opportunities to go deeper into our learning by giving us the ability to consume, and, more importantly, to create. As Joseph Joubert eloquently said, "To teach is to learn twice."[3] Now, more than any other time in history, people have this opportunity to "learn twice" by connecting and sharing with an audience.

21st CENTURY SCHOOL OR 21st CENTURY LEARNING?

A school with all the latest technology may well be a twenty-first-century school—modern in every way—and still not offer twenty-first-century learning. If we are only accessing the same information that previously existed in textbooks and handing in assignments with this technology, computers are no more than the equivalent of $1,000 pencils. It reminds me of the old Mel Brooks movie, *Blazing Saddles*. The town's citizens set up a fake town as a diversion for the bad guys. Then, with one gust of wind, the whole thing falls down and leaves the community at risk. The change was cosmetic. In the same way, throwing a bunch of high-tech devices into a classroom, with no shift in mindset on teaching and learning, is cosmetic. There's no depth, no real change.

Michael Fullan, researcher and former dean of the Ontario Institute for Studies in Education, said, "Learning is the driver; technology is the accelerator." Although I agree with this statement, if we do not understand the learning opportunities we have in front of us *because of technology*, we run the risk of accelerating learning outcomes that may not be relevant to the learner. Decisions should be made with the focus on learning, but we need to understand what opportunities are available for learning in today's world.

I also suggest that we adapt Fullan's statement to "*learners* are the driver; technology is the accelerator," and shift the onus onto the learners and empower them to take control of their own learning.

Technology gives us the power to accelerate, amplify, and even recreate learning. We, as educators and leaders, can make the most of these new opportunities by embracing the role of learner. Immersing ourselves in the learning process will give us a much better understand-

IMMERSING OURSELVES IN THE LEARNING PROCESS WILL GIVE US A MUCH BETTER UNDERSTANDING OF THE OPPORTUNITIES TECHNOLOGIES BRING TO OUR STUDENTS.

ing of the opportunities technologies bring to our students. Focusing on the learner, not just the learning, shifts the focus to a larger moral imperative to embrace the opportunities to educate and empower the students in our schools and classrooms in powerful ways.

IS TECHNOLOGY "JUST" A TOOL?

"Technology is just *a tool."*

I have been guilty of making that statement far too frequently in my career. In retrospect, I believe that throwing "just" in the phrase makes technology sound optional at best. Technology can actually be transformational, and it provides opportunities that didn't exist before.

You may have seen some of the online videos of people who hear sounds for the first time after receiving a hearing aid. One of my favorites is called "Lachlan's First Hearing Aid."[4] The little boy receives his first hearing aid at seven weeks old, and you can literally see wonder light up his eyes when he hears people speaking. The adults in the room become emotional because of what technology and someone's applied ingenuity have provided for this little boy.

I do not need a hearing aid, but Lachlan does. This technology is *transformational* to him and, really, that's all that matters for Lachlan.

Watching this video made me rethink the phrase "technology is *just* a tool." It also taught me, that, too often, we try to use technology to frame our teaching, when we should be trying to understand the opportunities it can provide for each individual.

TECHNOLOGY SHOULD PERSONALIZE, NOT STANDARDIZE.

#InnovatorsMindset

Technology should personalize, not standardize. The light that technology brought to Lachlan's eyes is something that many of our students have lost, due in large part to the formulaic process of school. We have more opportunities to create that light in our students' eyes than ever before. For example, students who have never felt comfortable speaking up in class may now feel free to share their voices through a different medium, such as videos, blogs, or podcasts. Other students who don't feel comfortable creating with their hands can now develop worlds through applications such as Minecraft or show their artistic side through web design or coding. The possibilities are endless.

LEARNER-CENTERED DECISIONS

Even when we have the best intentions and desire to teach the way our students learn, sometimes we fall back on what is easy, known, or comfortable—for us. Years ago, our school district issued a Blackberry mobile device to every administrator. The purpose was simply access; the leadership wanted to make it easy to contact people in case of an emergency. At the time, the majority of the administration team did not have or want a mobile device. One principal emphatically stated he would long be dead before he would carry a phone with him everywhere he went. (This person is still alive and has his own iPhone.) Fast-forward several years, the Blackberry was still the device of choice, not for the administrators but for the instructional technology (IT) department.

This hurts me as a Canadian to say, but the Blackberry wasn't a great learning device, especially compared to what the Android or iOS operating systems provided at the time. Blackberry focuses on serving business needs. The IT department, as well as our administrators, had grown comfortable with its features and many of them were reluctant to explore what other mobile technologies provided. Neither was there much initial interest in providing mobile devices for our students. After all, the thinking went, why would you want students answering phone calls or emails in the middle of class? Those attitudes began to change when we started to experiment with other mobile technologies like iPads and iPhones. The *learning opportunities* we experienced helped us view the possibilities for our students in a much different way.

The point of this illustration is not about choosing the best mobile devices. It is about the necessary shift in thinking regarding the learning opportunities technology provides for our students. Once educators started experimenting with these devices, they saw how learning experiences significantly changed and how they could create new, different, and *better* opportunities for our students.

Unfortunately, school-provided smart phones too often get relegated as "work phones." When that happens, educators may miss out on endless possibilities that the technology offers for us—and our students. Worse yet are the devices that are purchased by schools and districts, only to be met with the response of "Now what?" by teachers or administrators. One central office administrator told me about a school that purchased 150 iPads because the price for each had been reduced by fifty dollars. She later received a call from a school principal who said, "We have just received our new iPads. Now what do we do with them?" In the world of education—where resources are often scarce—not understanding the potential of a device leaves us continuing with traditional learning but at a higher cost. Let's take the time to understand what is possible from a learner-centered point of view, instead of blindly buying technology then asking "Now what?"

LEADING, LEARNING, AND SHARING

As a district, we understood that, if we wanted to see technology being used in powerful ways, we needed to help teachers see and experience the learning in new ways. With this in mind, we started the "Learning Leader Project." The project was an adaptation of a program we'd seen another organization successfully use to teach educators about technology by providing the opportunity to apply to attend twelve learning sessions. After attending all twelve sessions, each participant received a personal laptop. We remixed the program's structure so that, in addition to allowing the attendees to explore the opportunities technology provided, they would also be encouraged to share

> EVEN WHEN WE HAVE THE BEST INTENTIONS, SOMETIMES WE FALL BACK ON WHAT IS EASY, KNOWN, OR COMFORTABLE—FOR US.
> #InnovatorsMindset

what they learned and develop their leadership in the process. Each person was required to share the learning from at least two of the sessions back at their own school. We also cut the sessions from twelve to six and traded the laptop for an iPad.

We asked every school in our district to send at least one person from their school to six sessions (they could send more if they were willing to allocate money out of their own budget, which many of them did). The criteria for the attendees was not that they were necessarily great with technology, but that they had a) an interest in learning about the opportunities that technology could provide and b) were teacher leaders in their own building. Two months before the sessions started, each participant was provided with an iPad so they could become comfortable with it prior to the learning experiences. They could use it however they liked—whether that meant they explored it themselves, played games on it, or let their own children at home use it.

The incentive was never meant to be the iPad; the program was intended to create learning and leadership opportunities. The iPad afforded them access to information and new opportunities for learning and leadership. And its portability and extensive range of apps, as well as the ability to create, made it fun and easy to share learning with others.

We chose not to focus on apps in the sessions. Since the range of teachers extended from kindergarten to grade twelve, focusing on apps was inappropriate for the group. No one wants to sit through a session that isn't specifically relevant to them. Instead, we explored the new opportunities for learning that were provided with the technology. Because we wanted the participants to take ownership of their learning and find their own way, we spent as much time discussing ideologies of education as we did exploring the relevant potential and power of technology. The reason? If educators can't answer "Why?", then they will never get to the "How?" and "What?".

We also wanted to create an environment where people learned from a variety of people, not just the person organizing the session. Whether it was watching YouTube videos, Skyping in with educators, or talking face-to-face, the focus was on how we could learn from each other. The experience deepened everyone's learning. And as Seymour Papert explains, teachers desperately need this opportunity to learn for their own sakes, not just so they can teach.

> *If I wanted to become a better carpenter, I'll go find a good carpenter, and I'll work with this carpenter on doing carpentry or making things. And that's how I'll get to be a better carpenter. So if I want to be a better learner, I'll go find*

*somebody who's a good learner and with this person do some
learning. But this is the opposite of what we do in our schools.
We don't allow the teacher to do any learning. We don't allow
the kids to have the experience of learning with the teacher
because that's incompatible with the concept of the curriculum
where what is being taught is what's already known.*[5]

Hence the title "learning leaders." Individuals were there to help
lead others, and, at the same time, they had the opportunity to change
their own mindsets about what learning could look like in today's
world.

The learning leaders themselves comprised a diverse group of
teachers. Each individual had a different level of comfort and expertise. The expectation at the end of the program was that every person moved forward, not that everyone reached the same point. And
because the participants internalized their learning and shared it at
their own schools, we saw a significant shift in the thinking and attitudes toward technology in many schools.

CHANGING COURSE

Tom Murray, state and district digital learning director for
the Alliance for Excellent Education, wrote an article on "10 Steps
Technology Directors Can Take to Stay Relevant," in which he pushed
the thought of the changing roles of our IT departments.

*The role of the typical school district technology direc-
tor has become obsolete. Speak with your average teacher in
many school districts in the U.S., and you'll find the technology department is better known for getting in the way than
for serving the educational needs of both staff and students.
Many technology departments, led by obsolete tech directors,
are inadvertently inhibiting learning. The mantra of "lock it*

and block it" no longer works in a 21st-century digital learning environment.[6]

Murray goes on to provide ideas on revamping IT roles, such as spending time with educators, both in and out of classrooms, leading professional development, and being leaders in innovation through the ideas that they create to serve students. We must create safe environments and remove barriers, so that we can spend less time on fixing stuff and more time on deep learning.

Thankfully, my division's IT department is focused on how to serve kids and educators to help innovation flourish in schools. To ensure that we were making our decisions based on the learning that we wanted to create for our students, it was imperative that we worked with these employees to empower them in creating the learning environments we wanted for our students.

Based on this notion, here are four questions that can help guide the work of IT departments and help shape the conversations about the decisions we make regarding students.

1. **What is best for kids?**—This is a question that should not just be asked of our IT departments; it should be the question that guides all of our work. For example, the mindset about blocking many social media sites is that doing so keeps the kids safe. But in the long term, what seems to be best for kids is to educate them to navigate a really confusing and fast-paced world, rather than leaving them to figure it out on their own. If you decide to open these sites, ask what work is happening in the classrooms to ensure that students have an understanding of digital citizenship and their footprint. It is easy to say, "Open the site," but, if we do so, it's critical that we work with kids to ensure their online safety. This question helps educational leaders, teachers, and IT members understand how they can help each other.

2. **How does this improve learning?** In the past, I have seen software programs pushed into schools, even though they were really

business applications. Maybe it's a matter of pushy software sales-people, or maybe it sounds financially responsible to use the same software for multiple purposes. If neither educators nor the IT department can articulate how a new program or software will improve student learning, we have to stop and ask why is it being pushed to all computers.

The question works when asked by the educator or by the IT department employees. For example, if a teacher went to a conference and saw some cool software that he now thinks should

 LEARNERS ARE THE DRIVER, AND TECHNOLOGY IS THE ACCELERATOR.

#InnovatorsMindset

be installed on all computers, that educator should be able (and required) to articulate to his IT department why it is essential for learning. It's fine to test programs out in one or two classes to see if it's valuable or relevant, but when a software or technology is touted as something *all* students should have, we need to be able to explain how it serves learning. If neither side can answer this question, we are wasting time and resources.

3. **If we were to do _____, what is the balance of risk vs. reward?** Many IT departments look at risk assessment and want the risk to be either low or, preferably, zero. With that being said, how often do we look at the possible reward associated with doing something? For example, many schools completely block Twitter. Admittedly, there is a risk of opening social media sites for our students. However, allowing access to such sites and you telling your community, "We trust you," can yield *huge* rewards. In addition to the relationships that are strengthened by your trust, you allow

students and educators to network and expand their learning opportunities. When assessing the risk of opening up YouTube, you must also consider the rewards of the learning opportunities that are available with the second-most used search engine in the world (Google is number one). In my opinion, we stand to gain more than we lose by opening the site—if you are intentional about working with and teaching your students how to use it to their benefit. Regardless, educators should be able to articulate the rewards, instead of just asking, "Why isn't YouTube open?"

4. **Is this serving the few or the majority?** This question is essential when we make any policies. For some reason though, we seem to go overboard when it comes to technology. If a kid stabs someone with a pencil, he might be writing with it again by the end of the school day. Yet if there's a cyberbullying issue with one student, some schools respond by blocking social media altogether. It seems like quite an overreaction. Any time a new policy or procedure is presented for an entire school, we must ensure it does not punish everyone for the mistakes of a few. Innovative environments should be built on trust, not the lack of it.

By asking these questions, conversations with your IT department leaders should be much richer. And the outcome of those open discussions will help you to provide endless opportunities for your students.

MOVING FORWARD

As we move forward, it is essential to ask the question, "What is best for *this* learner?" Remember, *learners* are the driver; technology is the accelerator. It is now more important than ever to embrace the notion that, in education, *we are all learners.* It's only when we are willing to constantly expand and evaluate our own thinking that we will be able to create the environments our students so deeply deserve.

QUESTIONS FOR DISCUSSION

1. How do you model and explore new opportunities for learning in your own practice?

2. What opportunities are you providing for informal learning, exploration, and "play" with new technologies in your organization?

3. How do you move from "standardized" to "personalized" learning opportunities for your students and staff?

NOTES

1. Marshal McLuhan, *The Gutenberg Galaxy: The Making of Typographic Man* (Toronto: University of Toronto Press, 1962).

2. Alec Couros, "Bea's Makeup Tutorial," YouTube video, 5:00, March 13, 2015, https://www.youtube.com/watch?v=FfBSvEMob5g.

3. Joseph Joubert, *The Notebooks of Joseph Joubert* (New York: New York Review Books Classics, 2005).

4 Toby Lever, "'Lachlan's First Hearing Aids Aged 7 Weeks Old. Our Gorgeous Baby Boy," YouTube video, 1:27, August 31, 2014, https://www.youtube.com/watch?v=UUP02yTKWWo.

5. Seymour Papert, "Seymour Papert: Project-Based Learning," *Edutopia*, November 1, 2001, http://www.edutopia.org/seymour-papert-project-based-learning#page.

6. Tom Murray, "10 Steps Technology Directors Can Take to Stay Relevant," *SmartBlogs*, January 7, 2013, http://smartblogs.com/education/2013/01/07/the-obsolete-technology-direc-tor-murray-thomas/http://smartblogs.com/education/2013/01/07/the-obsolete-technology-director-murray-thomas/.

CHAPTER 10
LESS IS MORE

Everything should be made as simple as possible but not simpler.

—Albert Einstein

The ability to simplify means to eliminate the unnecessary so that the necessary may speak.

—Hans Hofmann

Have you ever received one of those extremely long work emails that has been cc'd to a minimum of ten other people? Were you excited about sifting through it to find out what (if anything) pertains to you? Probably not. More likely, you skimmed or maybe clicked DELETE without even reading it. In a world where we suffer from information overload, less is definitely more.

When asked about what he thought business schools should teach their students, Guy Kawasaki explained why less can be more when it comes to communication:

They should teach students how to communicate in five-sentence emails and with ten-slide PowerPoint presentations. If they just taught every student that, American business would be much better off.

No one wants to read War and Peace *emails. Who has the time? Ditto with sixty PowerPoint slides for a one-hour meeting.*

What you learn in school is the opposite of what happens in the real world. In school, you're always worried about minimums. You have to reach twenty pages or you have to have so many slides or whatever. Then you get out in the real world and you think, "I have to have a minimum of twenty pages and fifty slides."[1]

More so than ever before, educational organizations need to focus more on *depth* than *breadth*. Quality should always override quantity. But that isn't what happens in schools where teachers feel inundated by new initiatives and a myriad of organizational objectives. When edu-

IF WE AREN'T INTENTIONAL, WE MAY PROMOTE CONFUSION AND BURNOUT, INSTEAD OF INSPIRING INNOVATION AND DEEP LEARNING.

#InnovatorsMindset

cators and organizations feel overwhelmed by the number of requirements they have to meet, the focus in classrooms tends to be on covering curriculum, rather than focusing on the learning and exploring concepts in depth.

The *less is more* rule is a good one for leaders to follow. If we aren't intentional, we may promote confusion and burnout, instead of inspiring innovation and deep learning. Before you add a new initiative, ask yourself: Is this adding or subtracting to the already full plates of the educators I serve? Is this new program or initiative going to help us achieve our vision and, specifically, what are the goals for how it will impact learning?

MISTAKES IN MOVING FORWARD

During my first year as a principal, I was pretty excited about all of the opportunities that technology provided my staff. I saw all the awesome websites and tools that were out there and thought we would be crazy not to take full advantage of all of that *free* stuff. I passed on to my staff anything that I could get my hands on. Twitter supplied countless links with articles about how to make education better, as well as tips and techniques that could be implemented in the classroom *right away*. I felt it was imperative to share the tips and tweets with my staff; I wanted to light a fire under my team so we could use *all* those resources and ideas.

Bad move.

The more I shared, the more I noticed how overwhelmed my staff seemed. The more choices I provided them, the less they did with each one. It was too much. I also noticed that the staff members who did embrace everything I shared were only scratching the surface of how these tools and ideas could impact the learning experiences for their students. Our school started to seem "garden variety." The practice had made us knowledgeable in all but masters of none. This was no one's fault but my own. I had simply given my team way too many options without a clear focus.

THE PARADOX OF CHOICE

One of my favorite TED Talks is "Paradox of Choice" by Barry Schwartz. He explains how living in a world with so much choice can make us miserable. In his book by the same title, Schwartz writes about the peril that choice leads us towards:

> When people have no choice, life is almost unbearable. As the number of available choices increases, as it has in our consumer culture, the autonomy, control, and liberation this variety brings are powerful and positive. But as the number of choices keeps growing, negative aspects of having a multitude of options begin to appear. As the number of choices grows further, the negatives escalate until we become overloaded. At this point, choice no longer liberates but debilitates. It might even be said to tyrannize.[2]

After that first overwhelming year, I started asking my staff, "If we could simply pick a few technologies that you could use in your practice, would you prefer that?" Over and over again, the strong consensus was, "YES! *Please!*" Many educators know technology is important; they just don't know where to begin. The same is true in many other facets of education. Think about it: How many school teams could easily name ten things that they have worked on in the last three years? With too many initiatives, we only scratch the surface and remember very little about the purpose of the latest approach, much less the reason that trendy technique was "a must" three years ago. If we're

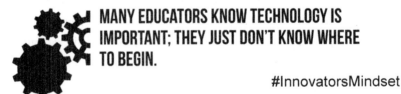

MANY EDUCATORS KNOW TECHNOLOGY IS IMPORTANT; THEY JUST DON'T KNOW WHERE TO BEGIN.

#InnovatorsMindset

going to go deep, rather than wide and shallow, we have to change the mindset that every new idea, even *good* ideas, must be immediately implemented. Instead of trying to do everything, let's focus on what we want learners to know and do and select and master resources to create

PROVIDE AMPLE TIME FOR EXPLORATION AND COLLABORATION TO ALLOW NEW AND BETTER IDEAS TO EMERGE.

learning experiences aligned with the vision that has been co-created with the community.

For example, with educational technology, educator Bernajean Porter's talks about the idea of moving from *literate*, to *adaptive*, to *transformative*. Using the iPad as an example, here is how those three areas break down:

- If I am *literate*, I am able to manipulate a device. I know how to turn it on, work with it, and turn apps on.
- If I am using the device in an *adaptive* way, I am doing something with this new technology that I used to do in low-tech way. For example, I am taking notes on the iPad or reading a textbook on the device.
- If I am using the device in a *transformative* way, I am doing something with the device that I could not do before, such as creating video, connecting with people around the world through a blog, or sharing items with other students in the classroom at any time, from any place.

When you attend a one-hour workshop that features "50 free tools," you will be lucky to hit the literate stage with each. Rather than empowering educators to push the boundaries of each tool's potential to impact learning, these broad sessions only scrape the surface of what is possible. Presenting fewer choices to your staff may seem counterintuitive, but doing so—and providing ample time for exploration and collaboration to allow new and better ideas to emerge—helps educators move to the point where the technology becomes transformative.

A FOCUS ON CREATION

They have to be interactive producers, not isolated consumers.

—John Seely Brown

Creativity is where we start to think differently, and *innovation* is where creativity comes to life. To me, the first goal is to get students to see themselves as creators because the real learning begins when students create. How many of us have ever been inspired by a teacher who simply writes notes on the board or has you fill in a worksheet? It's hard to be excited by copying down information that you are expected to regurgitate. The learning happens when we take what we know and make something out of it.

Creation is something we should strive for with our students' learning as well as with our work as educators. In all aspects of education, what we learn is not as important as what we *create* from what we learn. A focus on doing less allows us the time to actually go beyond surface-level learning and to really explore, so we can build a knowledge that enables us to move forward and innovate.

 **CREATIVITY IS WHERE WE START TO THINK DIFFERENTLY, AND INNOVATION IS WHERE CREATIVITY COMES TO LIFE.**

#InnovatorsMindset

In the video "Creativity Requires Time," elementary students were asked to complete a drawing of a clock in only ten seconds. Because the students felt rushed to create something, the final products all looked pretty much the same (two hands in a circle with the minutes marked inside), with really no creativity in the process. The students were then given ten minutes to complete the exact same task. This time, the drawings were much more creative and ranged from everything to clocks on a cat, a kite, and even people. The video reveals that "creativity is not inspired by the pressure of time," but the time to explore and to create was paramount in being successful at creating something new.[3]

This concept of allowing adequate time can and should be applied to the work we do as educators. If we are to move from repetition to creation and meaningful action, then the time allotted must be adequate. We are less innovative when our learning is thinly spread over a myriad of "initiatives."

A COMMON PURPOSE

Learning does not stop for two months at the end of one grade and then start on a new path at the beginning of the next grade. Learning does not happen in chunks; it is ongoing, non-linear, and continuous. This has always been true, but with the thoughtful use of technology, we can create a visibility of the learning our students do that was never able to happen before. With the tools we have access to, it is much easier to help students connect the real world to learning objectives, so they can apply that knowledge and create new ideas.

After my first year as principal, we narrowed the focus and selected three tools that would allow us to collaborate and share ideas locally and globally. With the goal of creating a culture of innovation, we chose tools that would empower us to learn, innovate, and meet the needs of our students. Those tools were:

1. **Google Apps for Education** to encourage communication both locally and globally.
2. **Blogs used as digital portfolios** to enhance and re-envision assessment.
3. **Twitter** to support professional learning and help develop personal learning networks.

With my own team, these three tools became part of our standard practice. By focusing on how to leverage the capabilities of these tools for every teacher in every subject, we have used them to transform the way we lead and learn. For example, we focused on using blogs to create portfolios because it was something that could be done by every teacher in every single class. Our blogs helped make learning visible and easy to share. An English teacher might choose to share his or her learning through writing posts. A physical education instructor may choose to use video to show skill development. Art teachers can post pictures of artwork, and language teachers may do a podcast about tips for learning a second language. All of these formats fit easily into our digital portfolios. More importantly, as educators became more comfortable with this tool in their own practice, it was much easier to understand the impact it could have on student learning.

 AS A LEADER, I WANT TO HELP UNLEASH PEOPLE'S POTENTIAL BECAUSE IT'S GOOD FOR THEM—AND BENEFICIAL FOR OUR STUDENTS.

You will notice, with each of the previous examples, that every teacher had a shared purpose that connected to larger goals. Each also has autonomy in the way he or she adds to this space. Author and motivation expert Daniel Pink explains why purpose and autonomy are crucial elements in each person's development. "Human beings have an innate inner drive to be autonomous, self-determined, and connected to one another. And when that drive is liberated, people achieve more and live richer lives."[4] As a leader, I want to help unleash people's potential because it's good for them—and beneficial for our students.

Side note: I mentioned earlier that our students also have a similar opportunity to create blog portfolios. With paper, a portfolio that moves from kindergarten to grade twelve would be impossible to manage. Technology makes it simple. We just have to recognize that we are all part of a child's development, a connection that is made visible in their blog portfolios. Likewise, we have to remember that this isn't a project that is will be completed in a month or a year. These long-term initiatives, like all change, require patience, perseverance, and focus.

ALLOW FOR EXPLORATION

Although offering too many choices can lead to feelings of becoming overwhelmed, it is imperative that leaders are careful not to constrain those we serve by *only* allowing them to explore designated tools or resources. The consistent use of tools can create innovation in their use, but if you do not encourage and model constant exploration, teaching practices can become stagnant. While I'm intentional about not bombarding my staff with ideas, I encourage them to seek out and try new things. After all, exploration and trial and error, even if they are messy, are often where powerful learning happens. If people believe they can go above and beyond what they are already doing, I want them to do so. The one thing I ask is that they share their expertise and new learning with others to help us collectively move towards our vision. Ultimately, as leaders, we must recognize, as we're adding what's important and removing what's unnecessary from our staff members' "plates," that every single person's plate size is different.

INNOVATION: UNIQUE TO EVERY SCHOOL AND CLASSROOM

Innovation, as we've discussed, should not be limited to technology integration. Rather, innovation should be a focus in any area that your school community deems important. Technology can be an accelerator for innovation in any program, whether it is health, robotics, or visual and performing arts. Based on your vision and your unique context, you'll want to come up with and implement ideas to make it part of your culture.

In an interview, Chris Kennedy, superintendent of the West Vancouver School District, told me his schools do not focus on initiatives but, instead, have "teacher innovation teams." Each team focuses on researching and developing ideas to help his school district to move forward. He reserves the term "initiatives" for things like infrastructure upgrades and bringing in technology. He focuses more on structures and directions when it comes to learning. As discussed in Chapter 8 on tapping into individual strengths, developing teams to lead in these few areas is more likely to be successful when the individuals are passionate about the focus area, as opposed to forced into leading something they are not interested in personally. Chris's commitment to innovation lies in three main areas for the organization: inquiry, self-regulation, and digital access. And, he stressed, each of those things looks different in different schools, which is where the magic happens. If we create "innovation teams" that simply make cookie-cutter versions of the same idea for every school and classroom, we neglect the most important component of innovation: empathy. In education, understanding the community we serve is critical and necessary for innovation to flourish in each of our unique communities.

BUT WHAT ABOUT THE BASICS?

Simplicity is about subtracting the obvious and adding the meaningful.

—John Maeda[5]

With all of this talk about "innovation" and "twenty-first-century learning" in organizations, some worry that the basic skills of literacy and numeracy will be forgotten. In fact, quite the opposite is happening in many organizations. Innovation demands that our students learn the basics, but how we go about teaching them may look different than in years past. The basics are crucial, but they cannot be the *only* things we teach our students. Yong Zhao summarized this nicely when I saw him speak at the 2012 ISTE conference, where he stated, "Reading and writing should be the floor, not the ceiling."[6] If we do not recognize

TECHNOLOGY CAN BE AN ACCELERATOR FOR INNOVATION IN ANY PROGRAM, WHETHER IT IS HEALTH, ROBOTICS, OR VISUAL AND PERFORMING ARTS.

and accommodate the shifts that are already happening in our world, we can forget about preparing kids for the future; we will not even be caught up to the present.

In 2010, Alberta Education (the government branch of education from the province of Alberta, Canada), started a focus on developing the whole child. The basics are at the core of learning in this approach, but they are only the beginning. Starting with the student in the center, the next focus is on the skills of literacy and numeracy. From there, education expands to discussing skills, such as collaboration and leadership, critical thinking and problem solving, creativity and innovation, social responsibility, communication, digital literacy, and lifelong learning.

So what could this look like in the classroom? Let's say students in an elementary class are writing in notebooks for their "journals" to promote reading and writing. The traditional practice has been that they write once, and, based on the size of the classroom, the teacher responding to all of the students may write fifteen to thirty times. The "whole child" approach might meet the same writing and reading goals by having students use their blogs as portfolios of their work. The students write their initial entries and are then encouraged to comment on five other classmates' blog entries. Instead of only writing once, the students are now writing at least six times, more when they respond to comments on their own blogs. They are still reading and writing (more than we ever had the opportunity to do as students), and, at the same time, they are developing a deeper understanding of collaboration, communication, digital citizenship, and critical thinking.

In education, time is the most precious and scarce resource. That truth makes it imperative that we create opportunities for students to learn more than one objective at any given time. Doing less—while intentionally getting better at what we are doing—is crucial. The example I shared above is one of countless ways that show how literacy is so much more than reading and writing. Blogging, sharing podcasts, and creating videos are just a few ways technology empowers educators to make the most of learning experiences. And each helps students master the basics, as well as the necessary practical and interpersonal skills that will equip them to learn from and communicate with others.

MOVING FORWARD

How would your staff members and students respond if someone asked, "What are the three big things that your school/organization is exploring?" Would they all say the same three things, or would you have double-digit objectives being shared? Along the same line, it's likely that most educators would find it easier to list the initiatives that have been added in the past couple of years than to list those that have been subtracted in the same time period. The constant addition of initiatives is leading many educators to feel burned out or leave the profession altogether.

As a school or system, when we limit our initiatives, tools, or techniques, we give ourselves time to discover what deep learning can really look and feel like. Focusing on a few key things promotes innovation in teaching and learning. And this sharp focus allows you to do

HAVING A LASER-LIKE FOCUS ON A FEW THINGS ALLOWS US TO GO DEEP AND PUSH OUR THINKING, WHILE CREATING NEW IDEAS TO MOVE FORWARD.

more—with less confusion, frustration, and stress. At the same time, by sharing those ideas and learning experiences with other teachers—within schools and around the world—you can help deepen understanding, allow for transformative learning, and disseminate ideas for innovation.

Ron Canuel, Canadian Education Association president and CEO, states that, "True innovation in education will only happen when a new structure is created: one that nurtures critical thinkers, supports risk-takers and encourages ongoing transformation, and that places a high value on creative and insightful learning / teaching in classrooms."[7]

If we are to create a system that nurtures the skills Canuel identifies, educators cannot feel like they are a "jack of all trades, master of none." Having a laser-like focus on a few things allows us to go deep and push our thinking, while creating new ideas to move forward.

Less should definitely lead to more.

QUESTIONS FOR DISCUSSION

1. What are the key areas that you and your community can focus on to bring your vision closer to reality?

2. How do you create opportunities and time for teams to lead in any specific area, and how will "success" be measured?

3. Moving forward, how could you lessen the "plate" of your staff and organization? What needs to stay and what needs to go?

NOTES

1. Adam Bryant, "Just Give Him 5 Sentences, Not War And Peace," *New York Times*, March 20, 2010, http://www.nytimes.com/2010/03/21/business/21corner.html.

2. Barry Schwartz, *The Paradox of Choice* (New York: HarperCollins, 2004), 2.

3. SimplyBest007, "Creativity Requires Time," YouTube video, 2:06, November 19, 2011, https://www.youtube.com/watch?v=VPbjSnZnWP0.

4. Daniel H. Pink, *Drive* (New York: Riverhead Books, 2009), 71.

5. John Maeda, *The Laws of Simplicity: Design, Technology, Business, Life* (Cambridge, MA: MIT Press, 2006), 89.

6. Yong Zhao, "Global, Creative, and Entrepreneurial: Defining High Quality Education," (keynote presentation, ISTE Convention) YouTube video, 1:15:59, June 26, 2012, https://www.youtube.com/watch?v=mKXeNKsjoMI.

7. Ron Canuel, "Innovation vs. Circulasticity: Why the Status Quo Keeps Bouncing Back," *Canadian Education Association*, November 2013, http://www.cea-ace.ca/education-canada/article/innovation-vs-circulasticity.

CHAPTER 11
EMBRACING AN OPEN CULTURE

The best way to have a good idea
is to have lots of ideas.

–Linus Pauling

I walked into the room and could tell right away.

I had never met the teacher, Jeff Unruh, before and knew very little about him, but the atmosphere in his classroom spoke of his commitment and passion. Turning to the colleague who was with me, I asked, "Do you think he is on Twitter?" I wanted her to make an educated guess, and her thoughts were the same as mine: *definitely.*

How did we know? Everywhere we looked, we could see the marks of connection, collaboration, and, yes, innovation.

Unique seating spaces and an environment that encouraged students to take risks and think differently gave clues of this teacher's values. Notices about "Genius Hour" and the school's recent "Maker Fair" were prominently displayed. And his class was learning how to play chess with a master player, who also happened to be a grandparent of one of the students.

Notice that I haven't mentioned anything about technology in this classroom. While students had access to computers, it was the learning environment that was different. It offered multiple, amazing opportunities for learning, tailored to reach students where they were and tap into their strengths and passions.

I asked the teacher if he was on Twitter, and he was, but he didn't share that much online. What he appreciated most was the information and people it gave him access to, and I could see how that information had been integrated to make his classroom look inviting and engaging. When I asked if he had noticed an impact on his classroom from using Twitter, he thought for a moment and likened it to the "boiling frog" anecdote; gradual input and changes had helped him get to where he was now. Just by being a "lurker" on Twitter, he'd been inspired to take small steps that made a noticeable difference.

Now, I am not saying that if you are not on Twitter, you are ineffective. Being on Twitter doesn't make you a great teacher any more than *not* being on Twitter makes you ineffective. There are a lot of great teachers who do some pretty amazing things despite choosing not to connect online. That said, having 24/7 access to great ideas and forward-thinking teachers through Twitter and other social media increases your interactions with others and provides access to new ideas. A network helps people become better. How could it not?

Looking at this teacher's classroom, I realized it looked *nothing* like my own when I first started teaching. Honestly, I did not have the access to the same information that teachers do now. I had the teachers in my school to bounce ideas off of, but compared to the global conversations that now occur every day, I was fairly isolated. Today, isolation is a choice educators make. Our connectivity and learning opportunities have changed in recent years, and, thankfully, many teachers are taking advantage of those changes to benefit themselves and, more importantly, their students. We have access to information and, equally valuable, to each other. We need to tap into that.

CALL ME MAYBE

I apologize for what I am about to do right now, but do you remember the song "Call Me Maybe" from 2012? Carly Rae Jespen's viral hit seemed to be all over the place. If you turned on the radio, there it was. If you went on to social media, there it was. It became, for many (including myself), a song that you hated yet knew all of the words to. There have been catchy songs before, but this spread quickly—not unlike a plague.

In addition to the song's catchiness, part of the reason for its success was that the audience did not simply listen to it, they recreated and remixed it. If you didn't like the original, you might have liked the version done by the Harvard baseball team in a van, Jimmy Fallon's version using instruments from an elementary music classroom, *Sesame Street*'s version involving Cookie Monster, or even the remix of President Obama singing every word of the song, which someone created by taking snippets from his speeches and aligning them with the song. I hated the song until I saw Jimmy Fallon's version, which appealed to the teacher side of me. After hearing it, I even purchased the original. The unique versions of the song somehow pushed listeners back to what the original artist had created.

The parodies and variations that are common today are quite a change from traditional copyright thinking. The old mindset of artists was, "If you copy or revise my work, you take away my opportunity to make a living." Now the ability to remix and reshare creates a culture where everyone can win. In Lawrence Lessig's TED Talk titled "Laws That Choke Creativity," he spoke about the difference between my generation (and those more seasoned than me) and the younger generations saying, "We made mixed tapes; they *remix* music. We watched

TV; they make TV."[1] And because that happens, professionals benefit from the mass sharing, and amateurs enjoy and learn from the ability to freely create. The lines between "amateur" and "professional" have blurred. Admittedly, some professional artists may see this blurring as

AS EDUCATIONAL LEADERS, WE MUST PROMOTE AND CAPITALIZE ON OPEN, CONNECTED LEARNING.
#InnovatorsMindset

a threat. In contrast, those with an abundance mentality know that this new era allows them to tap into different people's unique strengths to create a more powerful product or brand.

So what does this have to do with education? Everything. As noted in Chapter 3, Chris Anderson, the entrepreneur who reinvented TED Talks, discussed the idea of "Crowd Accelerated Innovation" in his 2010 TED Talk. Pointing to the example of dancing, he noted that the ability to see dancing through videos has accelerated people's skills, as well as the popularity of the art form. YouTube makes it possible, he notes, for people to be self-taught. And at the same time, the visibility it provides has raised the bar for excellence. Anderson even acknowledged that seeing great talks by others inspired TED speakers to create more powerful talks. He noted three key elements to "Crowd Accelerated Innovation:"

1. **People who share a common interest.** "The bigger the crowd, the more potential innovators there are.... They're creating the ecosystem from which innovation emerges."

2. **Visibility to see what others are doing.** "You need clear, open visibility of what the best people in that crowd are capable of because that is how you will learn, how you will be empowered to participate."

3. **Desire to change, grow, and improve.** "Innovation's hard work. It's based on *hundreds of hours of research, of practice.* Absent desire, [it's] not going to happen."[2]

Jeff Unruh, the teacher I mentioned at the beginning of this chapter, significantly changed his practice in a short time because he was a beneficiary of all three of these things.

1. He connected with other educators not only in his school and district but also through social media (the crowd).

2. Their ideas were shared openly (visibility), and he was able to disseminate what would work best for the community he served.

3. Ultimately, his intention (the desire) to become better pushed him to make his classroom the innovative environment that his students needed.

Ralph Waldo Emerson said, *"Nothing great has ever been achieved without enthusiasm."*[3] Jeff exemplified that in spades.

Liz Wiseman and Greg McKeown explain in their book, *Multipliers*, "It isn't how much you know that matters. What matters is how much access you have to what other people know. It isn't just how intelligent your team members are; it is how much of that intelligence you can draw out and put to use."[4]

So whether it is developing better dancers, creating or remixing music, or designing a better classroom experience, the more open we are, the more likely something amazing will come out of it. Innovation expert Steven Johnson, says, "We can think more creatively if we open our minds to the many connected environments that make creativity possible."[5] As educational leaders, we must promote and capitalize on open, connected learning.

HOW DO I HELP MAKE GREAT LEARNING GO VIRAL?

When I first moved into administration, a conversation with Carolyn Cameron, my former assistant principal when I was a teacher, shaped the way I worked. She told me that her role in administration had helped her become a better educator because she now had the opportunity to see great teachers teach all of the time. She also learned by watching practices that were not strong. She was right. I quickly learned that the best way to become a better educator is to have access to other teachers. I made sure that I went into classrooms every single day to observe and absorb what great educators do. The flexibility of my role, like Carolyn's, made it easy to observe other teachers. But budget and time constraints didn't afford my teachers the same opportunities. The question that kept going through my mind was: *How do we make great learning go viral?*

Shortly after a conversation with Will Richardson, a provocative thought leader in education (who I did not know at the time), and my own brother, Dr. Alec Couros, also an educator, I realized something had to change. I had told them about some of the technologies I had discovered in some of the classes I had observed, and Will asked me how I was sharing those powerful examples of teaching and learning with my staff. I told him that I wasn't, and he simply said, "So you are not into sharing?" His question (which was really a statement) challenged me to stop hoarding what I had learned from so many great educators.

Instead of keeping this information to myself, I began to share, on Twitter and my own blog, the things I saw in classrooms on a regular basis. The open platforms meant that these stories were not limited to our schools. As mentioned previously, people around the world read about the idea of "Identity Day." As I tweeted to our school and community about some of the amazing things I had seen during this opportunity, people in other cities and countries took notice and asked questions. Social media is *not* meant to be another form of email, but, as my brother would say, more like dipping your cup into a stream of information. You do not need to keep up with everything. By simply being in the space, the best ideas will make their way to you.

Our Identity Day had a tremendous impact on student learning and relationships. Why would I want to keep that experience to myself? I decided I couldn't. And in the spirit of "Call Me Maybe," people took the ideas and stories I shared and remixed them to meet the needs of their communities—whether it was to get to know their students better or to promote students being good to one another. As others shared and revised the idea, students around the world benefited. And as our leaders saw how others created their own Identity Days, we found ways to revamp and tweak the original concept. After a while, people weren't sure where the idea originated, but that doesn't matter. What's important is that the idea helped create a positive difference for kids.

In Chapter 4, I noted the difference between classroom teachers and school teachers. The Internet makes it possible to take a powerful step further to *global* teacher. The ideas you share have the potential to make an impact not only on your students but on kids around the world as well. If this is true, why don't more teachers share what they're learning and how they're teaching? I've heard many educators say, "I have nothing great to share." My response to that is always, "Well then, how are you meeting the needs of your students?" I'm not trying to make educators feel badly, in fact, quite the opposite. My intent is to help these teachers see that what they are doing, even if it seems commonplace to them, could be extremely helpful or insightful to someone else. Derek Sivers illustrates this point in a beautiful, short video titled, "Obvious to You. Amazing to Others."[6] (Go watch it on YouTube.)

If you compare your first few years in this profession to now, you may not initially notice how radically your teaching and learning styles have changed. Like Jeff Unruh, our practices change gradually over time. But if you stop to really consider what you've learned, you might shake your head at some of your past practices—and be thankful for, maybe even impressed by, your progress and growth. I know that's true for me. And ten years from now, what you know and how you think will be different, not simply because of your personal and professional growth but because of the new opportunities that the world will continue to provide. My encouragement to you is to share your learning every step of the way, so others can benefit from your experience.

THE ACCELERATION OF LEARNING AND LEADERSHIP THROUGH SHARING

Sharing your learning helps others, but it also benefits *you*. Every time I write a blog post, I think deeply about what I'm sharing because I know others will read it. I want to make sure I am sharing great stuff. In Chapter 3, I referenced Clive Thompson's *Wired* article, "Why Even the Worst Bloggers Are Making Us Smarter," which noted the value of having an audience. In the same piece, Thompson also shared that, although much of the writing posted on the Internet each day through social media and email (the equivalent of 36 million books a day at the time of his article) is not Shakespeare quality, the mere fact that we are writing more has changed the way we think and is "accelerating the creation of new ideas and the advancement of global knowledge."[7] What really pushes our thinking is not consuming information, but reflecting, creating, and sharing our ideas with the understanding that others will read it. The more we connect, the more opportunities will come our way. And as Steven Johnson said in his 2010 TED Talk, "chance favors the connected mind."[8]

If we, as leaders, want to accelerate our own growth, rather than just encourage others to do so, we must actively participate in the sharing of ideas. That is why in 2011, with the help of Patrick Larkin, then-Burlington High School principal and currently associate superintendent in the same school district, I created Connected Principals (connectedprincipals.com). The site is a place where leaders can share and collaborate with other school administrators. It fulfills a two-fold purpose: *accelerating* our own learning and leadership and *modeling* the willingness to constantly grow as individuals. We also use the hashtag #cpchat (Connected Principals Chat) to make the shared ideas more visible on social media and to act as a "bat signal" for administrators who needed help. Having access to 24/7 support from other school administrators is something I have greatly appreciated and taken advantage of, and the power of this kind of connection is not limited to school administrators. Whatever you teach, there is probably a hashtag for it. Whether it is science (#scichat), kindergarten (#kinderchat), or French immersion educators (#frimm), you have the ability to learn from and share with people around the globe.

COMPETITIVE COLLABORATION

Creating an open culture promotes both collaboration and competition. Alone, these concepts may be detrimental—too much collaboration does not necessarily bring out the best in us, and too much competition can isolate us—but *competitive collaboration* in an open environment can accelerate innovation.

COMPETITIVE COLLABORATION IN AN OPEN ENVIRONMENT CAN ACCELERATE INNOVATION.

#InnovatorsMindset

Here is when competition is harmful…

School "A" is competing with school "B" for students. Because of that, neither is willing to share what they are doing—their *trade secrets*—with the competition.

I see two problems with this mindset. The first is, if you aren't sharing your best ideas because you're trying to gain a competitive advantage, you may be harming yourself. If no one knows you are doing anything great, why would they come to your school? The second and more disturbing problem with this secrecy mindset is that the focus is not on helping kids but helping ourselves.

But *competitive collaboration* can be an accelerator. Here's an example: Two high schools in the same district used the same hashtag to show and share their work. The collaboration between the schools was beneficial to the teachers and, more importantly, the students. The competition came when one of the schools did an activity that the other school was not doing and the kids (at both schools) thought it was amazing. Not wanting to be outdone, students at the other school took the idea, improved it with some tweaks, and posted their work. Both of these schools are more than willing to help one another, and neither wants to be outdone. Who is the ultimate winner of this competition? The kids. *Competition* is only a bad word in education if our students lose out as a result.

When we view "sharing" as something that both supports and pushes us to be better, the big winner will always be our students. When leaders, educators, and learners commit to serving one another in an open environment, everyone's opportunities for deep and powerful learning can grow exponentially.

GO GLOBAL, IMPACT LOCAL

The opportunity to share on a global scale also has the power to break down walls *within* schools. In the busy-ness of any school day, it is hard to dedicate time to professional learning. Using a hashtag is a simple way to create connections between teachers in our own buildings. Tony Sinanis, principal of Cantiague Elementary School in Jericho, New York, embraces the opportunity that sharing has created to connect with his own school and models this openly through his Twitter account (@TonySinanis) and school hashtag #Cantiague. Anyone, including his staff, can check out this hashtag and see what educators in his school are doing in the classroom, books and blogs they are reading, and what students are writing and vlogging (video

WHAT IF ALL TEACHERS TWEETED ONCE A DAY ABOUT SOMETHING THEY DID IN THEIR CLASSROOMS AND TOOK FIVE MINUTES TO READ OTHER TEACHERS' TWEETS?

blogging) about for the school newsletter. *The hashtag is not about communication as much as it is about community.* Tony embodies this community spirit by communicating in a manner that is not "top-down;" he shares as an active member in this space. His example models the reality that we can learn from anyone, no matter their position.

The simplicity of a school or district hashtag can be even more meaningful than simply sharing events at the school. Think about this: What if all teachers tweeted (using their school's hashtag) about one thing a day that they did in their classrooms and took five minutes to read other teachers' tweets? Imagine the positive impact that simple action would have on learning and school culture. I have experienced the benefits of this practice firsthand. My own school district uses the hashtag #PSD70. By sharing and reading what others in their school community have to say, people have come to know one another on a deeper level, even though we are spread over almost one hundred miles.

Surrey School District, the largest school district in the province of British Columbia with more than 71,000 students and winner of the 2015 ISTE Sylvia Charp Award for District Innovation in Technology, has dispelled the myth that the rate of change needs to be slow within large organizations. Using social media platforms, like blogs, Instagram, and Twitter, and by staying connected to one another with the hashtag #sd36learn, they have shifted practices significantly within their school district in the areas of technology, assessment, and collaborative learning environments. As a side benefit, this connection enables a small-town feel during their learning events.

Culture is often not something you can measure. Rather, it's something you can feel. During the past few years, I've had the pleasure of consulting with leaders and teachers in the Surrey School District, and I've seen the passion, excitement, and love the leaders and staff in this district exhibit for learning and for one another. This is not to say they still do not have their struggles; significant growth and change is never completely comfortable. However, the leaders in this district have accelerated the opportunities for themselves and others by maintaining a strong focus on the value of sharing.

MOVING FORWARD

Our world today is participatory; sharing should not be the exception in education but the rule. Whether it is remixing "Call Me Maybe," learning how to dance, or transforming your teaching practice, technology today gives you the ability to *create, share,* and *connect.* As leaders within our communities, schools can no longer ignore this cultural shift; we need to accelerate it. Sharing is a necessity for our growth as individuals and as an industry, and, I promise, *you* have something worth sharing.

I want to note, too, that the use of technology does not lessen the value or impact of face-to-face connections. In fact, if we use technology to share on a consistent basis, face-to-face connections will likely improve. Teachers from other schools in the same district may only see one another every few months (if that), but when they have constant access to each other online, they stay *connected*. Being able to see what is happening within our own schools by using a common hashtag could also enrich the conversations in the staff room. Imagine what saying, "I saw your tweet about what you did yesterday... can you tell me more about it?" would do for both the learning and the relationships of your faculty.

In an open culture, the opportunities for learning and relationships are endless. The biggest winners of this sharing revolution are our students. We simply need to embrace what lies at our fingertips.

QUESTIONS FOR DISCUSSION

1. How are you actively sharing your learning with your school and global community?

2. How do you make great learning go "viral" in your school and move from "pockets" to a "culture of innovation?"

3. How do you use the concept of "competitive collaboration" to accelerate the growth of individuals and your school/organization as a whole?

NOTES

1. Lawrence Lessig, "Laws That Choke Creativity," TED Talk, 18:56, March 2007, http://www.ted.com/talks/larry_lessig_says_the_law_is_strangling_creativity?language=en.

2. Chris Anderson, "How Web Video Powers Global Innovation," TED Talk, 18:53, July 2010, http://www.ted.com/talks/chris_anderson_how_web_video_powers_global_innovation?language=en.

3. Ralph Waldo Emerson, "Circles," in *Emerson: Essays and Lectures* (New York: Literary Classics, 1983).

4. Liz Wiseman with Greg McKeown, *Multipliers: How the Best Leaders Make Everyone Smarter* (New York: HarperCollins, 2010).

5. Steven Johnson, *Where Good Ideas Come From: The Natural History of Innovation* (New York: Riverhead Books, 2010).

6. Derek Sivers, "Obvious to You. Amazing to Others," YouTube video, 1:54, June 28, 2011, https://www.youtube.com/watch?v=xcmI5SSQLmE.

7. Clive Thompson, "Why Even the Worst Bloggers Are Making Us Smarter," *WIRED*, September 17, 2013, http://www.wired.com/2013/09/how-successful-networks-nurture-good-ideas-2/.

8. Steven Johnson, *Where Good Ideas Come From: The Natural History of Innovation* (New York: Riverhead Books, 2010).

CHAPTER 12
CREATE MEANINGFUL LEARNING EXPERIENCES FOR EDUCATORS

The only source of knowledge is experience.

—Albert Einstein

Staff meetings were something I dreaded as a teacher. It seemed we often spent the majority of our time together discussing and debating rules and policies. It pains me to think about how many hours have been wasted talking about whether kids should or shouldn't wear hats in school.

I saw the following quote on a slide and have shared it many times in talks I have given to leadership groups. It seems to resonate with many: "If I die, I hope it's during a staff meeting because the transition to death would be so subtle. #Relevant"

As shared in Chapter 5, if you want to be innovative, you have to disrupt your routine. Watching a PowerPoint presentation on "twenty-first-century learning," rather than actually *experiencing twenty-first century learning* seems counterproductive. Lecture has its place in learning, otherwise TED Talks would not be so popular. But if lectures and traditional staff meetings are the only way we try to improve the profession, we are more likely to maintain the status quo than move forward. Bruce Dixon, an educational thought leader from Australia, said something to me that challenged the way I think about and plan learning experiences for educators. He explained that, "In no other profession in the world do we watch someone do it for sixteen years and then do it ourselves." But in teaching, that's exactly what happens. Teachers learn how to teach by watching their teachers. We often create what we experience, which means that to change what happens in our schools, the experiences we create in our professional learning must first change.

Professional learning is often viewed as a singular event, rather than a constant part of our development as learners. This traditional approach to professional development is not sufficient to help most educators shift their practice, and, as a result, rarely changes learning

WE OFTEN CREATE WHAT WE EXPERIENCE, WHICH MEANS THE EXPERIENCES WE CREATE IN OUR PROFESSIONAL LEARNING MUST CHANGE.

#InnovatorsMindset

for students. In most cases, the procedures and policies still convey that we expect teachers to "learn and do," rather than engage in ongoing activities that foster learning as part of a teacher's work day. To truly integrate new learning, it is critical to carve out time for exploration, collaboration, and reflection to allow educators to apply what they are learning. It is the application of the new learning that breeds innovative ideas and practices that work for your unique context and begin to make an impact for the learners across schools and classrooms.

CREATING OUR OWN LEARNING OPPORTUNITIES

Scott McLeod, founding director of the UCEA Center for the Advanced Study of Technology Leadership in Education, argues that educators focus far too much on discussing teaching, and not enough time is spent immersing ourselves in powerful learning and modeling it for others:

> We're supposed to be about learning in schools, right? How many schools have a mission or vision or purpose statement that says, "Blah blah blah lifelong learning blah blah blah?" 97 percent? 99 percent? 100 percent? And yet we do a terrible job of modeling this as educators (and parents).
>
> How many of us purposefully and explicitly model the learning process for our children? How many of us stand up in front of kids and say, "This is what I'm learning right now. I'm not any good at the moment, but this is the process I'm following, and this is what my plan is for achieving success. And I'll give you an update in a few weeks, and then another few weeks, and so on, about how I'm doing?" How many of us purposefully and explicitly show our students what it means to struggle with learning, overcome obstacles, and emerge on the other side more skilled and more knowledgeable than we were before? You already know the answer: nearly zero.
>
> There are many reasons why we don't model the learning process as adults, but one of the biggest ones is ego. We feel like we have to be the "experts" instead of co-learners. Administrators can show no weaknesses in front of teachers. Teachers and parents can show no weaknesses in front of children.
>
> What would our kids gain from us if, as educators and parents, we did a better job of showing that we too are learners? What would schools be like if the adults in the building

purposefully and explicitly lived and shared the process of being a learner? What would education be like if we adults intentionally created opportunities to be co-learners with the children that we serve?[1]

McLeod's position is especially relevant in today's world, where anything we want to learn about is at our fingertips. Yes, schools will still have the responsibility to elevate all, but there should also be opportunities for all learners (child and adult alike) to drive their own learning. The ability to learn at any time, any place, and at any pace is the reality of our world, and it's something that has changed the way I view my own professional learning practice. Will Richardson, co-founder of Modern Learner Media, encourages educators to jump in and take advantage of the same opportunities for learning that our kids do every day. "Truth be told, teachers should be responsible for their own PD [professional development] now. Kids wouldn't wait for a blogging workshop. Adults shouldn't either."[2]

If you want students to use Google Apps for Education in the classroom, use it with your staff. If you want learning to be personalized for students, help personalize it for staff (and yourself). This experience helps you and your staff embrace change and allows you to experience what students will feel in the classroom. Likewise, creating opportunities for educators to learn in the same spaces and environments that our students experience daily is important because it helps to build an empathetic viewpoint of the possibilities for learning today. Separating spaces where adults learn from where students learn is counterproductive. It is hard to become innovative in any practice without having a basic understanding of ourselves; fluency starts with literacy.

8 THINGS TO LOOK FOR IN TODAY'S PROFESSIONAL LEARNING

Understanding the learning opportunities that we would like to create for our students begins by immersing ourselves in similar learning experiences. Let's look back at the "8 Things to Look for in Today's Classroom" model and consider how we can apply it to professional learning. I've included the graphic created by Sylvia Duckworth again for reference.[3]

Review the following suggestions for ways you can create a culture of professional learning in schools and districts. I've shared an idea for each of the eight elements, but, obviously, each idea can have multiple elements or opportunities. I encourage you to look at these suggestions as a starting point and then create your own solutions that are personalized to you and your staff.

VOICE

Rationale: Creating opportunities for educators to share their ideas with others openly can lead to the "crowd accelerated innovation" that we discussed in the previous chapter. Empowering only a few voices generates ideas from only a few people, which does not take advantage of the ability that we have to flatten our organizations in today's world. Sharing their voices openly also helps educators to be more cognizant of their digital footprints.

Idea: One of the tactics I have experimented with in the past year is using video reflections. Twitter's 2014 release of the ability to post thirty-second videos inspired me to initiate #EDUin30, where I would ask a question through a thirty-second video prompt, and others from around the world would reflect and respond. Some people leave their own video, but others, who may not be comfortable with that format, can easily tweet a picture, a blog post, or any other type of media, and then tag it with #EDUin30. The experiment has helped me tap into the "wisdom of the room" and could have a major impact on the culture and community in which everyone is respected as both a teacher and a learner.

Thought leader and former school administrator Kelly Christopherson suggests having teachers do a monthly TED-style talk during staff time. The short presentations could be used to share something the teacher is either learning or trying in the classroom with students.[4] Such an opportunity would promote innovation by empowering educators to share what they are doing with others in their organization.

Other elements that could be incorporated: Reflection, Connected Learning, Self-Assessment, Critical Thinking.

CHOICE

Rationale: "Owning" one's own learning helps ensure that the learning actually happens. Still, much professional learning is delivered from top-down and decided upon for individuals. Allowing people to explore their passions is more likely to lead people to go deep and embrace what they have learned. They'll also be more inclined to share their knowledge and apply it in innovative ways. Simon Sinek states, "Working hard for something we don't care about is called stress; working hard for something we love is called passion."[5] When people are learning something about which they are passionate, the challenge is well worth the effort.

Idea: EdCamp has been sweeping the entire world and is a great way for educators to have ownership of their learning. Sessions are developed, created, and led by the educators who partake in the event. Because the people in the room are passionate about the topic, the conversations are rich and deep with learning. The EdCamp format is

 WHEN PEOPLE ARE LEARNING SOMETHING ABOUT WHICH THEY ARE PASSIONATE, THE CHALLENGE IS WELL WORTH THE EFFORT.

something that could (and should) happen during professional learning days. The pushback on this idea is that leaders and educators don't have time to prepare for and coordinate it. But if "learning" is the priority of the school, creating time and opportunities for deep learning should be the norm, not the exception.

Other elements that could be incorporated: Voice, Reflection, Critical Thinking, Opportunities for Innovation, Problem Finders/ Solvers.

TIME FOR REFLECTION

Rationale: Reflection is powerful for learning and for personal growth. And it's something that should be embedded into all of our professional learning. Although collaboration is an important process for growth of an organization, people need time to process ideas and thoughts. Learning is deeply personal, and without reflection time and having the opportunity to connect your own ideas and personal learning to what is being shared, it is harder to go deep into ideas or retain and share them.

I reflect, therefore I learn.

Reflection is necessary at every level of education today.

Idea: One of the practices I use at my workshops is to share ideas and some of my reflective thinking and then give the participants an extended break with reflection time embedded into it. Something as simple as a Google Form can provide a place for people to process their thoughts, while simultaneously tapping into the power of open reflection. Knowing that one's thoughts will be visible to the others in the workshop encourages people to think more deeply about the ideas

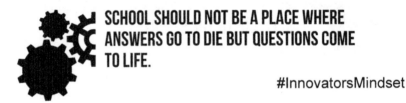

SCHOOL SHOULD NOT BE A PLACE WHERE ANSWERS GO TO DIE BUT QUESTIONS COME TO LIFE.

#InnovatorsMindset

that they are about to share. (The same is true on a global scale for blogs and social media sharing.)

In my workshops, I often use the following simple questions to encourage reflection:

1. What is something you learned about today that you would like to further explore? Why do you want to explore that topic?

2. What is one big question you have moving forward?

3. Any other thoughts that you would like to share?

An important element of this reflection is asking people to not only share their thoughts but to ask questions. Asking questions is essential to learning and reflection; they drive us forward. School should not be a place where answers go to die but questions come to life.

Other elements that could be incorporated: Voice, Self-Assessment, Critical Thinking, Connected Learning.

OPPORTUNITIES FOR INNOVATION

Rationale: If we want innovative students, we need to focus on becoming innovative educators. As with all elements shared for professional learning, it is essential that we allow our staff (and ourselves) ongoing opportunities to learn and develop our practice. "Innovation" is a process, and those willing to try new ideas need time to experiment and make them better.

Idea: My good friend and assistant principal of Greystone Centennial Middle School in Spruce Grove, Alberta, Jesse McLean, promotes the idea of "Innovation Week" for his students (an iteration of "Innovation Day" started by Illinois teacher Josh Stumpenhorst). During this week, students submit a proposal for something they want to either create or solve and are then given class time to go through the process. Jesse knew that if this initiative was to be successful, educators would have to partake in a similar process. So he developed the idea of "Educator Innovation Day." This day gives teachers time to tinker and develop innovative ideas both inside and outside of education.[6]

Chris Wejr has created innovation time through "Fed-Ex Prep," an idea inspired by Daniel Pink. He covered a class for teachers to allow them the time to create and work on ideas to share with others the next day.[7] Another idea is to adapt Google's famous "20% time," allocating time for self-directed work that would benefit both students and other staff members.

None of these ideas have to be taken as-is but can be adapted to fit the communities we serve. What is (again) crucial to the success of developing educators into innovators is putting a priority on innovation and devoting the necessary time to the process. Developing innovators and entrepreneurs is essential to the forward movement of our schools; we need to create professional learning opportunities that promote "innovation" as a necessity, not a luxury. As Yong Zhao, presidential chair and director of the Institute for Global and Online Education at University of Oregon, notes, "If something is missing, we need to create it. In this case, if there are no entrepreneurs, we need to make some. And to make some is to instill the entrepreneurship spirit into our children from the outside through education."[8] And that education begins with innovative, entrepreneurial-minded teachers and leaders.

Other elements that could be incorporated: Critical Thinking, Choice, Connected Learning, Problem Finders/Solvers.

CRITICAL THINKING

Rationale: In a world where information is abundant, it is important for our students to be able to critically evaluate information and understand their own thoughts and biases. Additionally, they must be equipped and encouraged to develop questions that challenge conventional wisdom.

Just as we look for critical thinking skills in our students, we must also promote it in meaningful ways in our professional learning. We need to create spaces and environments where we can assess, push, and consider ideas through critical discourse, if we are to move forward as individuals and as a whole. If schools are ever to be truly innovative, leadership must be open to having people question, even challenge, current practices. Remember: a flattened organization allows this type of thinking to thrive.

Idea: So many of the ideas shared throughout this chapter provide opportunities to challenge the conventional wisdom of professional learning. As I stated earlier, these are not prescriptive ideas but my own thoughts on how we can revamp professional learning. I encourage you to talk with your staff, establish your own criteria on what successful professional learning looks like and then develop new ideas on how it could be implemented. I would love to see a similar process implemented on an individual basis, where staff share what they believe successful personal learning to be and then provide a plan on how to implement it.

The goal is to challenge the notion of "we have always done it this way." Using the process of inquiry-based professional learning, the challenge could start with the prompt of, "Why do we… ?" For example, questions that could be explored might be, "Why do we have student awards?" or "Why do we use report cards as our main assessment tool?" Not every question needs to start with "Why?" They could also be along the lines of, "Does the process of school impede deep learning?" The point is to challenge the assumptions that we have about the process of school.

The value of this inquiry process is that you'll start to look at ideas with fresh eyes. Encouraging your staff to ask questions and actively research new ideas and solutions are crucial steps toward innovation in school. Positive change is more likely to happen within an organization when its people are active contributors to the process.

Other elements that could be incorporated: Opportunities for Innovation, Voice, Choice, Problem Finders/Solvers.

PROBLEM FINDERS/SOLVERS

Rationale: As referenced in Chapter 3, developing students into problem solvers and problem *finders* is crucial for their success. If we are going to ask students to find and solve problems in the classroom, it is essential that we do the same in our work. How often are we put in situations where we are asked to identify and solve problems in pursuit of creating better opportunities for our students? The short answer is, not enough.

The messages of the "I Learn" visual by Krissy Venosdale should not be reserved solely for our students. It is for everyone involved in education; we must all be learners.[9] Thinking, questioning, designing, creating, struggling, collaborating, trying, solving, inventing, reflecting, and learning are all crucial characteristics of the problem finder/solver. They are practices we should use at both the individual and organizational level.

Idea: The process for inquiry-based learning emphasizes not only solving problems but also formulating questions to find those problems in the first place. Below, I've included Alberta Education's process of inquiry-based learning for students. Read it, and then we'll look at how it could be adapted for educators:

Effective inquiry is more than just asking questions. Inquiry-based learning is a complex process where students formulate questions, investigate to find answers, build new understandings, meanings and knowledge, and then communicate their learnings to others. In classrooms where teachers emphasize inquiry-based learning, students are actively involved in solving authentic (real-life) problems within the context of the curriculum and/or community. These powerful learning experiences engage students deeply.[10]

With some simple tweaks, this can be created as a powerful statement in how we think about professional learning so that we can improve the opportunities we provide for students:

*Effective inquiry is more than just asking questions. Inquiry-based learning is a complex process where ~~students~~ **learners** formulate questions, investigate to find answers, build new understandings, meanings and knowledge, and then communicate their learnings to others to create real solutions to improve learning and the environment of the classroom(s) and school. In ~~classrooms~~ **a school** where ~~teachers~~ **administrators** emphasize inquiry-based learning, ~~students~~*

staff members are actively involved in solving authentic (real-life) problems within the context of the curriculum and/ or community. These powerful learning experiences engage and empower students and staff deeply.

Whether it is moving to Bring Your Own Devices (BYOD), developing Makerspaces, or starting any new type of program, staff and students need to be involved in the change process. By challenging the way schools function and empowering our communities to devise and act upon their solutions, our organizations can move forward while modeling the type of learning we want to happen in our classrooms. How often are teachers, students, and your community actively involved and empowered in the change process? I encourage you to commit to empowering the people you serve to be part of the process of finding and solving problems.

Other elements that could be incorporated: Critical Thinking, Voice, Choice, Opportunities for Innovation.

SELF-ASSESSMENT

Rationale: School has been set up in a way that makes us dependent upon someone else to tell us how we are doing. This is true for students (report cards), as well as with the evaluation process for educators. One of the many problems with a system that depends on someone else to affirm or correct our progress is that students will encounter bad teachers, teachers will encounter bad principals, and principals will encounter weak superintendents. When the evaluator/ leader is not strong, the system is ineffective, even detrimental. By contrast, having an understanding of your own strengths and weaknesses is hugely beneficial not only in education but also in every area of life—personal or professional.

Idea: Blogs as digital portfolios offer an opportunity to showcase learning, as well as time for reflection. Maintaining my own digital portfolio during the last five years (through my blog, georgecouros.ca) has helped me grow more than almost any other professional learning opportunity. I've connected with other leaders and educators, sharpened my communication skills, and reflected on what and how I have learned. An added bonus is that I have been able to document and evaluate my learning process over time, so I can easily see my own growth.

INCLUDING A DIGITAL PORTFOLIO AS PART OF THE (SELF-) EVALUATION FLIPS THE CONVERSATION FROM WHAT THE EVALUATOR SEES TO WHAT THE EDUCATOR SEES.

Having educators create their own portfolio allows us to shift the focus of the conversation from the "evaluator" to the "learner." For example, in traditional evaluations, observations are shared from the viewpoint of the administrator to a teacher. Conversations can be started from these types of evaluations, but, from my experience, the focus (and the talking) comes from the evaluator far more often than it does from the teacher. Including a digital portfolio as part of the (self-) evaluation flips the conversation from what the evaluator sees to what the educator sees. You can simply start by asking a question such as, "Where are you strong, and where do you need to grow?" With their portfolio in front of them, your staff members will be able to reflect on and evaluate their progress, strengths, and weaknesses with you.

Dean Shareski offers a few insights on how blogging develops better educators.

Thousands of other blogging educators could echo similar words. In fact, I've yet to hear anyone who has stuck with blogging suggest it's been anything less than essential to their growth and improvement... If you look at the promise of Professional Learning Communities (PLC) that our schools have invested thousands, more likely millions, to achieve, blogs accomplish much of the same things. The basic idea of the PLC is to have teachers share practice/data and work in teams to make improvements. A good blog does this and more. While the data may not be school specific, great bloggers know how to share data and experience that is both relevant and universal, so any reader can contribute and create discussion.[11]

Putting an emphasis on self-assessment benefits the individual learner, and when shared openly on a blog, it benefits other educators as well. The more transparency we have in our learning and practices as educators—both inside and outside our organizations—the more we can tap into one another to drive positive change.

CONNECTED LEARNING

Rationale: The opportunities for learning in our world today are immense. *Not only do we have free and immediate access to an inexhaustible wealth of information, but we also have access to one another.* The simple ability to connect provides major benefits for the learning environment of our students. It also enables us, as leaders and continual learners, to accelerate and amplify powerful learning opportunities for ourselves and those we serve.

Dr. Alec Couros (full disclosure, he is my brother) created "The Networked Teacher" image to illustrate what connected learning and teaching involve.[12]

Although the technologies identified and how they're used can change, the most important part of this illustration, in my opinion, are the arrows that go back and forth. Networked educators are both *consumers* **and** *creators* of information. These connections accelerate innovation and allow educators to create better opportunities for our students.

Idea: If connected learning is valued as something that makes an impact on the learning for students, we must prioritize time for

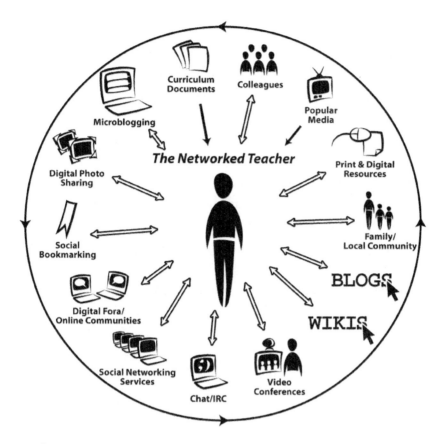

teachers to connect with local and global colleagues during the work day. This should include opportunities for educators to connect with their professional learning networks (PLNs) to address their specific interests and questions. Pointing them to resources such as the Edublogs Teacher Challenges, "Where educators are stepped through weekly tasks that increase their skills while being supported by mentors,"[13] is one way to help them get started with online connections.

Developing the habit of connecting is the first step. Rather than, or, perhaps, in addition to doing Google searches for a teaching tool or strategy, ask the same question on Twitter—and remember to use a hashtag that will make the tweet easy to find. You just may get better results, and you'll be making the shift from literacy (basic understanding) to fluency (learning how to leverage the technology). You'll also be establishing powerful connections.

Speaking of hashtags, anytime I deliver a keynote or workshop for educators, I always share a hashtag where they can connect and learn from one another in real time. My belief is that if the participants are only learning from me, they may miss out on incredible opportunities to learn from one another. The same is true within your school or district. As I mentioned in Chapter 11, using a hashtag can accelerate learning and foster a sense of community. Using a hashtag throughout the year, not just during professional learning events, allows you and your staff the ability to capitalize on both synchronous and asynchronous learning. (It's also one more way to collect evidence of growth throughout the year.)

Other elements that could be incorporated: Reflection, Voice, Choice, Opportunities for Innovation.

MOVING FORWARD

What I wanted to provide in this chapter was not the answer to professional learning but suggestions to help spark ideas. You may choose to use something you've read here as-is, or you may want to tweak or completely revamp an approach. As a leader in your own organiza-

> IF YOU'LL GET COMFORTABLE WITH PEOPLE LEARNING AT DIFFERENT PACES, YOU'LL HELP THEM REACH THEIR HIGHEST POTENTIAL.

tion, it is important that you build upon what your community knows and where it needs to go to grow. What is essential for the success of any professional learning opportunity is to recognize that people need to move from *their* point A to *their* point B. Learning doesn't happen by simply distributing information. As Paulo Coelho, author of *The Alchemist*, notes, "People never learn anything by being told; they have to find out for themselves."[14] That means learning for staff should be personalized and empowering. As a leader, it can be frustrating to feel as if your staff is all over the place, but if you'll get comfortable with people learning at different paces, you'll help them reach their highest potential.

QUESTIONS FOR DISCUSSION

1. How do you both personalize learning opportunities while moving the co-created vision forward for your school/ organization?

2. How do you create connections to the learning that we do as educators to the opportunities that are created for students in your school? Are you creating what you experience?

3. Which elements of the "8 Things to Look for in Today's Classroom" do you already see in your professional learning opportunities? What elements are lacking?

NOTES

1. Scott McLeod, "Blah Blah Blah Life Long Learning Blah Blah Blah," *Dangerously Irrelevant* (blog), May 23, 2011, http://dangerouslyirrelevant.org/2011/05/blah-blah-blah-life-long-learning-blah-blah-blah.html.

2. Will Richardson, "More To It," *Will Richardson: Read. Write. Connect. Learn* (blog), May 23, 2013, http://willrichardson.com/post/51144392972/more-to-it.

3. George Couros, "8 Things to Look for in Today's Classroom," *The Principal of Change: Stories of Leading and Learning* (blog), January 8, 2013, http://georgecouros.ca/blog/archives/3586.

4. Kelly Christopherson, "5 Ways To Empower Educators," *Educational Discourse: Learning – A Dialogue with Others* (blog), July 15, 2015, http://kellychristopherson.ca/wp/archives/2379.

5. Simon Sinek, Twitter post, February 28, 2012, 4:20 a.m., https://twitter.com/simonsinek/status/174469085726375936.

6. Jesse McLean, "Innovation Week- Contraint," *Jesse McLean: Opening Doors and Turning on Lights* (blog), September 14, 2014, http://jessepmclean.com/tag/innovation-week/.

7. Chris Wejr, "Creating Time for Teachers to Meet and Tinker With Ideas #RSCON4," *Connected Principals: Sharing. Learning. Leading.* (blog), October 9, 2013, http://connectedprincipals.com/archives/9144.

8. Yong Zhao, *World Class Learners: Educating Creative and Entrepreneurial Students* (Thousand Oaks, CA: Corwin, 2012), 93.

9. Image used with permission: Krissy Venosdale (@venspired), "Make School More," *Venspired.com*, February 23, 2014, http://venspired.com/make-school-more/.

10. Alberta Education, "Inquiry Based Learning," *Alberta.ca*, n.d., https://education.alberta.ca/teachers/aisi.aspx.

11. Dean Shareski, "How To Make Better Teachers," *Ideas and Thoughts: Learning Stuff Since 1964* (blog), November 18, 2010, http://ideasandthoughts.org/2010/11/18/how-to-make-better-teachers/.

12. Image used with permission: Alec Couros, "Examining the open movement: Possibilities and implications for education." 2006 Doctoral Dissertation, University of Regina, Regina, SK, Canada. http://www.editlib.org/p/118036/.

13. Edublogs, "Edublogs Teacher Challenges," *Edublogs.org*, accessed September 19, 2015, http://teacherchallenge.edublogs.org.

14. Paulo Coelho, *The Alchemist* (New York: HarperOne, 1988).

PART IV: CONCLUDING THOUGHTS

CHAPTER 13
ARE WE THERE YET?

Organizational wisdom transcends
organizational learning in its
commitment to doing the right
things over doing things right.

—Martin Hays[1]

L et's do a recap of what we have so far.

In Part I, we defined innovation, discussed why it is important in education, and identified the characteristics of the innovator's mindset.

In Part II, we focused on laying the groundwork for innovation in education by developing relationships, modeling what we seek, empowering our people, and creating a vision for learning *with* our community, rather than for it.

In Part III, we looked at how to unleash talent in our school communities and create the conditions that allow for innovation to flourish. Creating the environment that fosters a culture of innovation is done by:

- focusing on strengths-based leadership,
- allowing learners' needs to drive our decisions,
- narrowing our focus and engaging in deep learning,
- embracing an open culture,
- and creating learning experiences for educators that we would love to see in the classroom.

It's important to note that the strategies listed above are not meant to be linear. All contribute to the innovative environments we hope to create. The questions on the next page will foster the implementation of each strategy. Take some time to review and answer these questions about how you are (or will begin) unleashing talent in your organization, schools, and classrooms.

The word *innovation* is becoming more prevalent in school and district mission and vision statements. Our job as leaders is to make sure that innovation isn't simply a word but a mindset that intentionally and consistently shapes our daily practice. Our actions, as I mentioned earlier, must align with our mission and vision statements. If we are still focused on solely doing well on standardized exams, then preparing students to be successful in the world today, and in their future, isn't really our chief concern. This is not to say that tests are irrelevant, but a testing culture is. As the old saying goes, you do not fatten a pig by weighing it. If we want our students to be designers, thinkers, creators, and leaders, we must first realize that having them regurgitate information on a piece of paper or even on a computer will achieve nothing more than compliance. I'm not saying that *everything* we did in school before—as teachers or even as students—was irrelevant. What I *am* saying is that we have the information, resources, and networks to create something much better.

Unleashing Talent	Driving Question(s)?	Your Answers
Strengths-Based Leadership	Do I know and build upon the strengths of those I serve?	
Powerful Learning First, Technology Second	Are we embracing new (and better) opportunities for learning, and making decisions based on supporting these new realities?	
Less is More	What are the few purposeful areas that we are focused on? How might we align our resources to support ongoing learning and development in these areas?	
Embracing an Open Culture	How do we share openly and regularly to further our own learning and development?	
Creating Meaningful Learning Experiences for Educators	Do our professional learning opportunities mirror the learning we want to create for our students?	

Look again at your answers to the questions in the chart. How might your school look or feel differently if you took immediate action in each of these areas? I believe you'll find that small changes may be enough to get things moving in a new and better direction.

A DIFFERENT TYPE OF ASSESSMENT

If we create a culture where every teacher believes they need to improve, not because they are not good enough but because they can be even better, there is no limit to what we can achieve.

—Dylan William

It is important to create evidence of the learning that is happening in our schools. In many schools, tests are the main measure of this evidence. Since that's the case, it isn't helpful for me to simply say a testing culture is bad without offering an alternative. I've already mentioned the initiative that has helped my own school division move forward and lessen the focus on standardized tests: digital portfolios. In previous chapters, I've explained a few of the reasons I encourage other educators to create digital portfolios. As we look at how to take steps toward improving education, I'd like to share just a bit more about how and why a school could and should use digital portfolios as part of the assessment process.

There are two main purposes that student and staff digital portfolios can serve. The first is that of a "learning portfolio," which shows the individual's growth over time. The second is as a "showcase portfolio," that highlights the person's best work. The easiest way to explain this is that, if you had a video of a student reading in September, October, November, and December, you could assess student growth over time, which is the benefit of a "learning portfolio." A "showcase portfolio" would show only the student's best sample (similar to a résumé). In this scenario, for example, the portfolio would include the video of the child's December reading as his "best work." If the process is genuine, the student, rather than the teacher, selects the "best work" to be showcased and explains the criteria for that selection.

In the traditional system, grading is subjective. What does an "A" mean in reading? Well, that depends on the grade level, the teacher or evaluator, and, sometimes, even the place where the assessment in being done. In contrast, a portfolio shows the actual learning and progress over time. It can also improve communication at home and between parents and teachers because it allows parents to see, in real-time, what their children are learning. Instead of asking, "What did you learn today?" and getting the traditional "nothing" response, parents can say, "I saw you did 'x' in science today... tell me more about it." This can create a much deeper conversation about learning with all stakeholders.

Here are four other examples of how online portfolios provide a better way to create evidence of and assess learning.

1. **A better opportunity to focus on "traditional" literacy.**

   Many people prefer portfolios to have links to examples of work, which is great for the "showcase" aspect. What I like about a blog is the opportunity to write, which is a hugely important part of the work students do in schools. There is a difference between having great ideas and having the ability to communicate those ideas. In our world, we need to be able to do both. As discussed in Chapter 10, a blog allows us to focus on the basics of reading and writing with students, perhaps even more so than traditional assignments because it provides multiple opportunities for practice and revision. And at the same time, students are honing their interpersonal communication skills. In short, the more we write, and read one another's writing, the better we become at writing.

2. **The ability to use a wide array of "literacies."**

Although reading and writing are important, it is essential that we create opportunities for both students and educators to have a voice. The reason blogs will always be beneficial is that, no matter what "medium" we want to use, we will have the opportunity to embed our new learning and ideas into the posts. If I want to write, I have that option. But if I want to make a video, create a Prezi, share photos, add a SlideShare, or do a podcast, I will be able to share it through my blog. We often evaluate students not on their understanding of a subject but on their ability to write about it. Blogs provide a variety of options that allow learners to use their strengths to communicate their mastery of content and desired learning objectives.

3. **The ability to develop an audience.**

As mentioned previously, having an audience can be invaluable to the learning process. When we create the "digital dumps" and put a bunch of links on a site, we are using this technology as a one-way medium, rather than an interactive exchange of ideas. Every time we share new content, blogging allows people to receive it through email subscriptions or RSS feeds. Students and teachers may not have tens of thousands of readers, but even an audience of ten can enhance the reflection experience. If you are going to take the time to create a portfolio, I think it is important to create content with the intent of sharing it. An audience is not only important for the potential connections you can make but is also beneficial in terms of collaboration. Through the comments and the ability for others to share ideas, this "audience" is important for true communication and the opportunity to connect with others who are interested in similar topics.

4. **Developing a voice.**

People are more likely to share their voice on something that they actually care about, whether that's photography, mechanics, cooking, dancing, Minecraft, fitness, skydiving, or a million different things. I have written more in the past five years than I ever did in school (kindergarten through university) because I have the freedom to write about what I want. Writing helped me develop my voice and share my thoughts. It pushed me to dive deeper into the things that I wanted to learn about. If you are going to start using blogs as portfolios with students, it is important to give them opportunities to share things that they care about, in addition to the required "school stuff." As an added benefit, you will learn so much more about them while helping them developing their voice. *If the freedom and opportunity to explore our passions works for us, why wouldn't it work for them?*

I'm not suggesting that digital portfolios be used in lieu of quantitative data. Rather, they can be used to provide some powerful stories that work in conjunction with other forms of assessment. Numbers are only a part of the story; written and visual examples of learning delivered from the student's point of view can improve our understanding of where we are and where we need to go. Additionally, digital portfolios provide opportunities for educators within an organization to see what students are doing in other classrooms, which can spark ideas and encourage competitive collaboration. If you want to see the effectiveness of an educator, you do not look at what the teacher is doing but at the learners whom they serve. This allows schools to tell stories about learning more than any number ever could.

IF YOU WANT TO SEE THE EFFECTIVENESS OF AN EDUCATOR, YOU DO NOT LOOK AT WHAT THE TEACHER IS DOING BUT AT THE LEARNERS WHOM THEY SERVE.

#InnovatorsMindset

A SHIFT IN LEARNING TO CREATE A SHIFT IN THINKING

As the use of digital portfolios grows in education systems around the world, technology companies are working to create the perfect app to meet this need. Even with the best tools, however, if we do not understand how a portfolio can impact our own learning as educators, we will not be successful in using this technology in a meaningful way for our students. Rather than accelerating learning, they will simply become the equivalent of a paper portfolio in a digital format. As discussed in Chapter 12, making portfolios part of our own practice as educators can help us fully appreciate the power of documenting and reflecting—all while communicating with and learning from an audience.

In Parkland School Division, we have used the Edublogs blogging platform for digital portfolios (although most blogging platforms could create something similar). We also use this platform for several other aspects of the work that we do on a continuous basis, including school blogs, classroom blogs, district communication, and group spaces where we share learning, such as our "Learning Coaches" initiative located at psdblogs.ca/learningcoaches. As discussed earlier, we began using portfolios so we could experience what we wanted to create. At the same time, this one platform helped to limit the number of tools used. By using the same technology as our students, our focus shifted from how to use the tool to how we can improve and enhance learning with it.

One of the ways we have used blogs is with an initiative called *184 Days of Learning* (psdblogs.ca/184), which showcased our learning for every day that students were in our buildings for the school year. The concept for this initiative was adapted from a group of educators in Atlanta who would daily ask their community, "What did you learn today?" We decided to pose the same question and created opportunities for our community to answer this question, no matter what role they had in our school districts, from students to our superintendent. The blog helped us see the impact of networked learning for ourselves and inspired ideas for powerful learning both in and out of our communities. Starting in 2011 and still continuing today, you can see the evidence of learning by our students, staff, and community. The blog beautifully illustrates the notion that we are all learners.

A favorite story of mine that happened when using the *184 Days of Learning* blog came from a student named Maddisyn, who wrote about a book called *The Dot*, by author Peter H. Reynolds. In her post, she writes a reflection about the beautiful message of the story:

> *I hope everyone gets a chance to read* The Dot *because, once you do, everything will seem a little bit different than it did before. I hope everyone in the whole world knows that they matter regardless of who they are and where they come from. It's important to know that even if you don't think you matter… You do!*[2]

Maddisyn shared an inspiring message with others around the world and is learning that her voice matters. Within twenty-four hours of her post being published, the author commented to Maddisyn (a grade four student at the time):

> *Maddisyn—Thanks for sharing your beautiful art! I enjoyed reading your thoughts about* The Dot—*and the connection between art and writing—and making your mark matter! Keep the creativity flowing! —Peter H. Reynolds*[3]

When I saw this comment, I was floored, as were Maddisyn, her teacher, and the other students who saw the author's comment. Maddisyn and our other students learned that day that each person's voice truly does matter. They also saw how the world is so connected today and that what we share can help and inspire others. Now, students in our school are being even more proactive about connecting—when they read a book, they ask, "Who is the author? What is his (or her) Twitter handle?" How many times have you had a similarly powerful experience from a standardized test (or the countless lessons spent preparing students for a test)? My conservative guess is… never.

HOW WILL YOU MEASURE SUCCESS?

We often try to use business metrics to measure the success of the school. Rather than counting money like a company does, we often use test scores to measure success. Sure, there are other metrics that help businesses determine future success, such as customer satisfaction, but the bottom line for almost any business is money; profit is a crucial measure. Although schools can learn from the business world, our success is not as quantifiable.

In a conversation with Katie Martin, director of professional learning for the University of San Diego's Mobile Technology Learning Center, she talked with me about the struggle schools face when it comes to determining whether or not they are successful. "Right now, we are at odds in many systems because we say we want kids to be critical thinkers, productive citizens, responsible decisions makers… and then we only measure 'success' by how they perform on a test and not celebrate how they have grown and developed the other desired skills and mindsets," she said. She's right. For years, we have taken the most human profession in the world and simply tried to reduce it to letters and grades, and it doesn't work.

Before we can decide if our schools are successful, we have to first define what success means, realizing our impact is measured long after a child leaves school. If you ask most adults about the school experiences that made a positive impact on them, it might have been a powerful project, a cool assignment, or a significant, positive relationship they had with a teacher who they might have felt was their "champion." Not any test.

So what does being successful mean? Many schools will share sta-
tistics regarding how many of their students go on to post-secondary
education, but if a student has a college degree and is unhappy in his
or her profession, do we deem that a success? Aside from academic
achievements, the success of a school should not only be measured by
what students do when they are in school but also by their impact on
the world after they leave the school environment. Even if a person

FOR YEARS, WE HAVE TAKEN THE MOST HUMAN PROFESSION IN THE WORLD AND SIMPLY TRIED TO REDUCE IT TO LETTERS AND GRADES, AND IT DOESN'T WORK.

earns higher degrees, makes a lot of money, and is happy, if he or she
isn't a contributing member of society, is that success? If not, is the
person or the schooling to blame?

Success is quite difficult to quantify, but like most aspects of education, we should consider it through the lens of our students. It would
be interesting to survey students after they leave school. Here are three
questions we could ask to help determine how we have done as schools:

1. Do you consider yourself as a successful, contributing mem-
    ber of society?

2. Why did you give the answer above?

3. What impact do you think school had on your answers?

The answers would not be in nice and neat little packages, but they
would tell us a lot about our schools' effectiveness. These three questions would not only give us some measure of how we are doing as a
school community, but the brevity of this survey makes it more likely
to be answered, while compiling some powerful qualitative data.

MOVING FORWARD

So, how do you know if your district, school, or classroom is "there" yet? The short answer is that you are not. We will never "arrive." This doesn't mean that you don't have the best school in the world; you very well might be fantastic. But since schools should be learning organizations that promote innovation, we must be constantly focused on improving our practice, which means we will never be done innovating, growing, and learning. Today's innovation could be tomorrow's norm—a reality that fuels a cycle of continuous improvement. Robert Sutton and Huggy Rao share how this focus of continual advancement is the norm for the best organizations all over the world:

> As Pixar's Academy Award-winning director Brad Bird puts it, organizations that spread and sustain excellence are infused with a "relentless restlessness"—that often uncomfortable urge for constant innovation, driven by the nagging feeling that things are never quite good enough.[4]

That "relentless restlessness" will serve our students well and empower educators as learners. If we ever stop learning, we might as well stop teaching. This book is not meant to give you the answers but to provoke more questions. It is also meant to spark conversations, not end them. I look at this book as a summative assessment of my learning as of the time it is published, but even this is not the end of my learning on this topic, only the beginning. If you think you are "there," you are already probably falling behind.

We have to develop a new understanding of what "better" looks like in the context of schools, especially with the ubiquitous access to technology that we have in our everyday lives. Dean Shareski implores leaders to rethink what success looks like in our world today:

> In the past decade, most everyone with access has experienced what it's like to learn from anyone, anywhere, at any time.

In everyday life, this is no longer an event to behold, but the way we learn. Any policymaker or leader who doesn't understand and live this needs to find other employment. I can't imagine people not being exposed to these ideas and shifts by now... This means new measures of success. Whether it's how well students communicate and tell stories using a variety of media, building and creating art, solving and finding real and current problems, collaborating effectively with people around the world, or writing code, there are infinite examples of doing better that are never going to fit inside a spreadsheet cell.[5]

As educational leaders and continuous learners, we must commit to perpetually moving forward, for our own sakes and for the benefit of the schools and the students we serve. Never stop asking questions or pushing the boundaries of what is possible for learning for our students and ourselves; this is where the true learning will happen.

QUESTIONS FOR DISCUSSION

1. How does your school community know that they are moving forward successfully towards their co-created vision?

2. How are you collecting powerful evidence of learning at all levels to showcase learning to each other and your community?

3. What are some of the questions you would ask students to learn more about their learning and experience in schools?

NOTES

1. J. Martin Hays, "Dynamics of Organisational Wisdom," *Business Renaissance Quarterly 2*, no. 4 (Winter 2007): 79.

2. Maddisyn (Millgrove School student), "Make Your Mark and Make It Matter," *184 Days of Learning* (blog), September 13, 2012, http://www.psdblogs.ca/184/2012/09/13/day-8-maddisyn-student-millgrove-school/.

3. Peter H. Reynolds, *Ibid*.

4. Robert I. Sutton and Huggy Rao, *Scaling Up Excellence*, (New York: Crown Business, 2014), xiii.

5. Dean Shareski, "Make It Stop," *The Huffington Post*, September 16, 2015, http://www.huffingtonpost.com/dean-shareski/make-it-stop_1_b_8142928.html.

CHAPTER 14
THE BIGGEST BARRIER AND "GAME CHANGER" TO INNOVATION IN EDUCATION

If your actions inspire others to dream more, learn more, do more, and become more, you are a leader.

—John Quincy Adams

An artist had his easel set up on a street when a person walked by and asked how much it would cost to have a portrait drawn "Fifty dollars," said the artist. The patron readily agreed, and the artist began to draw. Ten minutes later, the artist completed a beautiful, creative piece. Even though the patron was very happy with the creativity and the high quality of the piece, she challenged the agreed-upon price.

"Something that took such a short time to create should not have the high price tag," she said.

The artist responded, "It took me ten years to be able to do it in ten minutes; you have never seen much of the work that I have done to be able to draw this picture so quickly."

I heard this story a while back, and, although I can't remember its source, the message resonates with me, particularly as I read article after article about the battle between the "basics" versus "innovation" in education. While it seems so many choose one side or the other, I find myself somewhere in the middle. Innovation in any area requires a fundamental understanding of basic concepts. To be a great musician, you must learn the basic concepts of music. The best writers in the world at some point learned how to read and write. The speed at which people learn the fundamentals varies from person to person, but every master first had to acquire the basic knowledge and competency.

The basics are essential in our modern world. We all know this. Believe me, even as someone who is passionate about innovation in education, I still cringe at spelling mistakes. I hate them. I want kids to know their times tables and not have to rely on a calculator for simple math. The basics are important, but we need to go beyond knowing to creating and doing. Understanding how to read and write doesn't make you a writer. By contrast, if you are a writer, it's a given that you know how to read and write.

The way we learn—and the way we teach students even the most basic skills—must reflect and capitalize on the technology, information, and people we have access to today. We can't base the way we teach on how we were taught because a) we have powerful opportunities at our fingertips, and b) the way many of today's teachers were taught wasn't effective for all students, even when we were in school.

When I think about my own educational experience, I know that from grade one until around grade seven, my marks were usually in the top three of all students in my classroom, and, still, I never felt smart enough because I wasn't "number one." Being constantly ranked in school led me to the Ricky Bobby belief that, "If you're not first, you're last." With that mantra, I put in minimal effort for the rest of my time as a student, was barely accepted to university, and struggled academically for years. I knew the basics but never really saw myself becoming anything. I never saw myself as a writer, mathematician, scientist, or as anything academic. I went to university because my parents made me go, not because I had an epiphany when I was six years old that I was going to be a teacher. My parents expected me to go to university, so I did. I floated around for four years and then finally decided to go into education. In total, it took me six years to earn a four-year degree.

So why did I do well in my first years of school? To please my teachers.

Why did I get through university? To please my parents.

And why did I become a teacher? Because I didn't really know what else to do.

For the first time ever, at about the age of thirty-one, I identified myself as an educator not by profession but by passion. Getting there took someone else tapping into my strengths and interests and helping me see my own gifts and passions. A few years later, at age thirty-five, was when I first saw myself as a learner. And now five years later, as I complete this book's final chapter, I see myself as a writer.

In eighteen years of school as a student, writing paper after paper, I never once saw myself as a writer. But when I finally began to explore my own passions and started to deepen my own learning, I discovered that I actually enjoy writing. And only after completing a book and almost 1,000 blog posts am I starting to see myself as a writer. I am thankful to have found a love for what I do. I don't see my work as a "job" but as part of my being. I want my staff and students to experience that beautiful feeling—hopefully much sooner in their own lives.

Did my experiences in school help me get here? Absolutely, and I am thankful to the many teachers who spent so much time helping me to create the opportunities that I have today. Without those basics being reinforced in my formal education, as well as at home, I would not be the learner I am today. The question I have, though, is why didn't I see my own passions and talents earlier? More importantly, as an educator, how do I help students see their gifts?

People regularly challenge my focus on innovation with the question, "But what about the basics?" I hope that, by now, you know that I want our students to know the basics—and so much more. My parents came to Canada not to provide us the same opportunities that they had back in Greece but to create something better. That is my drive as an educator; to create a better version of school than what I experienced. I appreciate my own teachers and want to build on what they have done. My hope is that the future teachers of the world will not recreate what this generation has done but make something far better that is relevant for that generation. Isn't that the wish of every generation? To do better than what we have done in the past.

What made the artist invest ten years developing the skill to draw a picture in ten minutes? My guess is that, at some point, he became inspired and *saw himself as an artist.* My desire is for schools to be a part of the spark that allows individuals to go beyond what school has traditionally expected. We have always celebrated our top academic students and touted them as being successful, but sometimes they walk out of school only being great at the game of school and not much else. We can be so much more as educators, a fact that Erica Goldson shared in her very powerful high school valedictorian speech in 2010:

> *I am graduating. I should look at this as a positive experience, especially being at the top of my class. However, in retrospect, I cannot say that I am any more intelligent than my peers. I can attest that I am only the best at doing what I am told and working the system. Yet, here I stand, and I am supposed to be proud that I have completed this period of indoctrination. I will leave in the fall to go on to the next phase expected of me, in order to receive a paper document that certifies that I am capable of work. But I contest that I am a human being, a thinker, an adventurer—not a worker. A worker is someone who is trapped within repetition, a slave of the system set up before him. But now, I have successfully shown that I was the best slave. I did what I was told to the extreme. While others sat in class and doodled to later become great artists, I sat in class to take notes and become*

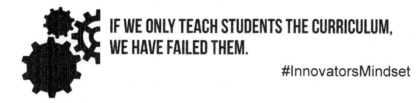

IF WE ONLY TEACH STUDENTS THE CURRICULUM, WE HAVE FAILED THEM.

#InnovatorsMindset

a great test taker. While others would come to class without their homework done because they were reading about an interest of theirs, I never missed an assignment. While others were creating music and writing lyrics, I decided to do extra credit, even though I never needed it. So, I wonder, why did I even want this position? Sure, I earned it, but what will come of it? When I leave educational institutionalism, will I be successful or forever lost? I have no clue about what I want to do with my life; I have no interests because I saw every subject of study as work, and I excelled at every subject just for the purpose of excelling, not learning. And quite frankly, now I'm scared.

We are more than robotic bookshelves, conditioned to blurt out facts we were taught in school. We are all very special. Every human on this planet is so special, so aren't we all deserving of something better, of using our minds for innovation rather than memorization, for creativity rather than futile activity, for rumination rather than stagnation? We are not here to get a degree, to then get a job, so we can consume industry-approved placation after placation. There is more, and more still.[1]

As Erica Goldson stated, there is so much more to our students, every single one of them. If we want to build on the strengths of our students, we need to develop them as learners who explore their passions and talents. For schools to do that, educators will need to unleash that talent and hunger for learning in themselves first. If we only teach students the curriculum, we have failed them.

MY STORY, YOUR STORY

This book offers only one viewpoint of a story of where schools could be. It's part of my story. But educators all over the world need to share their stories, as well, because stories inspire us all to move forward. As stated in Chapter 4, to inspire meaningful change, we have to make a connection to the heart before we make a connection to the mind. Sharing our stories about our learning and the ways we empower students helps us make the emotional connections that drives change. If I *feel* something, I am more likely to change my behaviors and beliefs than if I'm simply acquiring facts. Stories can become the fuel to innovation in education. I hope you'll share yours.

The majority of educators embrace this profession and the hard work it requires because they love their students. If we reduce what we do to numbers and letters to measure our achievements, then we forget that it is (or should be) passion that drives us. That is why our stories are so important, and it's why I want to encourage you to talk about the ideas you've read about in this book and have conversations. Build upon the ideas here and create new and better ones. Share your stories and insights on Twitter using the #innovatorsmindset hashtag. This way, we all can become a part of the narrative in how we can create better learning environments for our students.

STORIES CAN BECOME THE FUEL TO INNOVATION IN EDUCATION.

#InnovatorsMindset

In a documentary on his life, Muhammad Ali shared what he believed to not only be the shortest poem in the world but one of the most powerful. Ali shared the poem as he spoke at a Harvard commencement speech:

"Me. We."

Innovation starts with us as individuals, but we will need all educators to work together and embrace the innovator's mindset if we are to create something better for our students.

THE BIGGEST BARRIER AND GAME CHANGER

I started the book with a story about my dad, so it's fitting that I close by sharing how my mother has inspired me. At the beginning of the book, I wrote that my parents embody the belief that "change is an opportunity to do something amazing." Ultimately, "amazing" starts with us. When we embrace new opportunities, even when they seem like obstacles, we can create something much better than what currently exists. Change is scary, and it can seem easier to stay with a "known bad" than take the chance on the possibility of a "great" new opportunity. Fear can make us reluctant, but it doesn't have to defeat us.

Throughout her life, my mom has proven that it's up to each of us to overcome fear and choose to do something amazing. When my mother decided to emigrate from Greece to Canada to create a better life, she had no idea if she would see her family again. She had only a grade six education, but she worked hard and, alongside my dad, built a business, and provided a life with more opportunities for my siblings and me than they ever had as children. I remember her taking lessons to learn how to read when she was in her fifties and sixties. She knew that being able to read and write would create opportunities, even though learning the basics would be a struggle. Now, at almost eighty years old, she constantly sends me emails, and it is amazing how she gets better with every single one. She has even learned how to make me feel guilty for not calling home more often, solely through the use of emoticons, which is impressive in and of itself. I save each email she sends to me in a folder; it is like my mom's own learning portfolio. I cherish each one.

In the last few years, I have watched my mom deal with so much adversity and come out strong. My dad passed away two years ago, and her only brother passed away a year after that. In many ways, the older we get, the more we seem to lose, yet my mom still goes out of her way to show me love, connect with me, and give me advice. With so little formal education, she is wise in so many areas where I need her to be. More than anything, her wisdom comes from her attitude towards the world. She sees light in not only situations but also in people, even when it would be really easy to see darkness. Although I am all about embracing change, I don't know if I could have done what she has done in her lifetime.

In relation to her positive attitude, I have been thinking about the challenges we face in schools. With budget restrictions, policies that don't make sense, and curricula that are way too static for a world that is constantly changing, we could just throw in the towel and be okay with the notion of the school of the past. But, like my mom who wanted more for her kids than what she had, I am hoping we can create something better for our students than what we grew up with. When we know better, we should do better. People challenge others to think "outside of the box," when we really need to think about how we can become innovative *inside of the box.*

IT IS NOT ABOUT SKILL SET; IT IS ABOUT MINDSET.
#InnovatorsMindset

When the six-second video app Vine came out, some people asked, "What in the world could you possibly do with six seconds?" Others said, "I wonder what I could do with six seconds?" It is not about skill set; it is about mindset. While some looked at the time constraint as a barrier, others saw the constraint as an opportunity. You choose your perspective. It's okay to ask questions. Just make sure your questions aren't really excuses in disguise.

Making innovation part of education does not depend on, and is not hampered by, the policies or the curriculum; it depends on us. I hear things like, "Well, we can't possibly do that because of our (parents, students, teachers, principal, lack of resources, government, etc.)." And then I go online and see that someone somewhere has succeeded in the goal, while facing the same adversity. In fact, their story and success is better *because* of the adversity.

Do you know why people love reading comics or watching movies about superheroes? It is not just because they stretch our imaginations, but because they do amazing things while overcoming adversity. The story becomes so much more compelling when it is not easy. Have you seen those shirts that say, "I teach… what's your superpower?" Showing up each day is a start, but it's not enough. Being a teacher is not a superpower; the *way* we teach is. It's the mindset you bring into the classroom and to your school that can help change the world.

I recently saw the quote: "Be the hero in your own story." I think of my mom, who taught me to always look in the light when all you can see is darkness, and who overcame so much adversity to give everything she has to her kids to create something better, while showing love and kindness to everyone she encountered. She's the hero in her story because she focused on what she had and what she could do with it; she didn't allow a lack of material resources to stop her from reaching her goals. That same mindset is crucial to the innovative educator.

I am thankful for my mom, and I am constantly reminded, by her and by my dad's example, that the biggest barrier to innovation is our own way of thinking. I am also reminded of the biggest game changer—and it *isn't* technology. The biggest game changers in education are, and always will be, the educators who embrace the innovator's mindset. These teachers and educational leaders look at change as an opportunity, not an obstacle, and they constantly ask: "What is best for *this* learner?" With this mindset, they provide new and better learning experiences for our students every single day. When we, individually and collectively, embrace that mindset, we can, just as my parents did for me, create enormous opportunities for our students and make education what it should be. I look forward to the change that lies in front of me and the opportunity to create something better for our students; I hope you do, too.

QUESTIONS FOR DISCUSSION

1. What is one thing that you are going to try immediately to help move closer to a new vision for learning?

2. What is one big question you have about something you would like to change in the traditional school model?

3. What's your story now, and what's the story you want to tell? How will you make this happen?

NOTES

1. Erica Goldson, "Speech," *America Via Erica* (blog), June 25, 2010, http://americaviaerica.blogspot.com/p/speech.html.

ACKNOWLEDGMENTS

Never in my life did I think I would write a book on my own. In fact, I still haven't, because there are so many people who have done so much to help me share my learning with the world.

First, I want to thank my superintendent Tim Monds and the entire Parkland School Division community. Their vision of being, "a place where exploration, creativity, and imagination make learning exciting and where all learners aspire to reach their dreams," is something they encourage for their students as well as their staff. This entire community encouraged me to pursue my dreams and supported me the entire way.

To Kelly Wilkins, who took a chance on someone who was ready to quit teaching because she saw something in me that I hadn't yet. She is the best leader I have ever known.

To my coaches and teachers, who taught me that leadership is not something to which you are entitled, but something you earn.

To Dave and Shelley Burgess who tapped into my strengths and told me that I should write a book that I want to write.

To Katie Martin who I emailed every chapter to and bounced ideas off. She challenged my thinking, all while giving me the confidence to keep writing.

To all of the educators around the world who share their knowledge and passion. Their ideas fueled so much of what was written in this book.

To my brothers Alec and Michael, and my sister Tina, who all make me smarter, but do it with love first.

This book, however is dedicated to three people.

To my dad, who taught me that "change is an opportunity to do something amazing," by taking so many risks in his life to create something better for his family.

To my mom, who is the most loving person I know and embodies what I want to be as a lifelong learner and as a person who loves unconditionally. Even though she didn't learn to read until she was an adult, I assure you that she will read every line of this book several times, whether she cares about the subject matter or not.

And to my beautiful wife, Paige, who is the best person and teacher I know. She doesn't just encourage me to follow my dreams, she pushes me to do so—just like she does with her students—with more kindness than any person I have ever known.

MORE FROM

DAVE BURGESS
Consulting, Inc.

Teach Like a PIRATE

Increase Student Engagement, Boost Your Creativity, and Transform Your Life as an Educator

By Dave Burgess

(@BurgessDave)

Teach Like a PIRATE is the *New York Times*' best-selling book that has sparked a worldwide educational revolution. It is part inspirational manifesto that ignites passion for the profession and part practical road map filled with dynamic strategies to dramatically increase student engagement. Translated into multiple languages, its message resonates with educators who want to design outrageously creative lessons and transform school into a life-changing experience for students.

P is for PIRATE

Inspirational ABC's for Educators

By Dave and Shelley Burgess
(@Burgess_Shelley)

Teaching is an adventure that stretches the imagination and calls for creativity every day! In *P is for Pirate*, husband and wife team, Dave and Shelley Burgess, encourage and inspire educators to make their classrooms fun and exciting places to learn. Tapping into years of personal experience and drawing on the insights of more than seventy educators, the authors offer a wealth of ideas for making learning and teaching more fulfilling than ever before.

Ditch That Textbook

Free Your Teaching and Revolutionize Your Classroom

By Matt Miller (@jmattmiller)

Textbooks are symbols of centuries of old education. They're often outdated as soon as they hit students' desks. Acting "by the textbook" implies compliance and a lack of creativity. It's time to ditch those textbooks—and those textbook assumptions about learning! In *Ditch That Textbook*, teacher and blogger Matt Miller encourages educators to throw out meaningless, pedestrian teaching and learning practices. He empowers them to evolve and improve on old, standard, teaching methods. *Ditch That Textbook* is a support system, toolbox, and manifesto to help educators free their teaching and revolutionize their classrooms.

Learn Like a PIRATE

*Empower Your Students to
Collaborate, Lead, and Succeed*

By Paul Solarz (@PaulSolarz)

Today's job market demands that students be prepared to take responsibility for their lives and careers. We do them a disservice if we teach them how to earn passing grades without equipping them to take charge of their education. In *Learn Like a Pirate*, Paul Solarz explains how to design classroom experiences that encourage students to take risks and explore their passions in a stimulating, motivating, and supportive environment where improvement, rather than grades, is the focus. Discover how student-led classrooms help students thrive and develop into self-directed, confident citizens who are capable of making smart, responsible decisions, all on their own.

Pure Genius

*Building a Culture of Innovation and
Taking 20% Time to the Next Level*

By Don Wettrick (@DonWettrick)

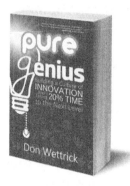

For far too long, schools have been bastions of boredom, killers of creativity, and way too comfortable with compliance and conformity. In *Pure Genius*, Don Wettrick explains how collaboration—with experts, students, and other educators—can help you create interesting, and even life-changing, opportunities for learning. Wettrick's book inspires and equips educators with a systematic blueprint for teaching innovation in any school.

50 Things You Can Do with Google Classroom

By Alice Keeler and Libbi Miller
(@alicekeeler, @MillerLibbi)

It can be challenging to add new technology to the classroom but it's a must if students are going to be well-equipped for the future. Alice Keeler and Libbi Miller shorten the learning curve by providing a thorough overview of the Google Classroom App. Part of Google Apps for Education (GAfE), Google Classroom was specifically designed to help teachers save time by streamlining the process of going digital. Complete with screenshots, *50 Things You Can Do with Google Classroom* provides ideas and step-by-step instructions to help teachers implement this powerful tool.

Master the Media

How Teaching Media Literacy Can Save Our Plugged-in World

By Julie Smith (@julnilsmith)

Written to help teachers and parents educate the next generation, *Master the Media* explains the history, purpose, and messages behind the media. The point isn't to get kids to unplug; it's to help them make informed choices, understand the difference between truth and lies, and discern perception from reality. Critical thinking leads to smarter decisions—and it's why media literacy can save the world.

The Zen Teacher

Creating FOCUS, SIMPLICITY, and TRANQUILITY in the Classroom

By Dan Tricarico (@thezenteacher)

Teachers have incredible power to influence, even improve, the future. In *The Zen Teacher*, educator, blogger, and speaker Dan Tricarico provides practical, easy-to-use techniques to help teachers be their best—unrushed and fully focused—so they can maximize their performance and improve their quality of life. In this introductory guide, Dan Tricarico explains what it means to develop a Zen practice—something that has nothing to do with religion and everything to do with your ability to thrive in the classroom.

BRING GEORGE COUROS
TO YOUR SCHOOL OR EVENT

George Couros offers engaging and empowering keynotes, workshops, and professional development programs. His insightful blend of research, personal stories, and practical advice for implementing new learning helps others feel comfortable in taking control of their own personal and professional growth. Having served at a variety of levels as an educator and administrator, George shares his personal experience and wisdom to equip educators and leaders to take risks that result in innovative learning opportunities for students.

WHAT PEOPLE ARE SAYING ABOUT GEORGE COUROS

"Great messages from George Couros. I'm laughing, I'm crying, I'm learning and thinking. Thank you."

"Uplifting, amazing, motivating presentation George Couros. Be the game changer and change the lives of your students!"

"George Couros... your words will be forever in my heart. You are an amazing speaker. I will be a better educator, wife, mom, and daughter due to this message."

" I think George Couros's keynote was the best I've ever experienced."

ABOUT THE AUTHOR

GEORGE COUROS is a leading educator in the area of innovative leadership, teaching, and learning. He has worked with all levels of school, from K-12 as a teacher and technology facilitator and as a school and district administrator. He is a sought after speaker on the topic of innovative student learning and engagement and has worked with schools and organizations around the globe. George is also the creator of ConnectedPrincipals.com, an initiative that brings educators and leaders together from around the world to create powerful learning opportunities for students.

Although George is a leader in the area of innovation, his focus is always the development of leadership and people and what is best for learners. His belief that meaningful change happens when you first connect to people's hearts is modeled in his writing and speaking. You can connect with George on his blog, "The Principal of Change" (located at georgecouros.ca) or through Twitter (@gcouros).

CPSIA information can be obtained at www.ICGtesting.com
Printed in the USA
BVOW06s1233061215

429477BV00008B/164/P

POPULAR MESSAGES FROM GEORGE COUROS

Although his presentations can be tailored to your event, here is a sample of keynote presentations that George has done in the past:

Leading Innovative Change

The Innovator's Mindset

Innovate. Create. Voice.

8 Things to Look for in Today's Classroom

Digital Citizenship to Digital Leadership (Student Focus)

Parenting in a Digital Age (Parent/Community Focus)

CONNECT

Connect with George Couros for more information about bringing him to your event.

 georgecouros@gmail.com

 @gcouros

 GeorgeCouros.ca